# HOW IT ALL

# VEGAN!

IRRESISTIBLE RECIPES
FOR AN ANIMAL-FREE DIET

## TANYA BARNARD & SARAH KRAMER

## Dedicated to

Sue Kramer, Art Kramer, and Dale Barnard

Published in 2008 by
Grub Street
4 Rainham Close
London
SW11 6SS
Email: food@grubstreet.co.uk
Web: www.grubstreet.co.uk

First published in Canada by Arsenal Pulp Press

A CIP record for this book is available from the British Library

ISBN 978-1-906502-072

Printed and bound in England by MPG Books Ltd, Bodmin, Cornwall

This book has been printed on FSC (Forest Stewardship Council) paper

**A note on flour and baking for this UK edition**

British plain flour has less protein (9.5-10%) than American all-purpose flour (9-11%), so best baking results may be achieved by using a mixture of half plain and half bread flour. Bread flour has between 12% and 13% protein, and helps produce wonderfully well-risen loaves of bread. Pastry flour is low-protein flour (8%-9%) and is used in making biscuits, cookies, pie crusts, and pastries. It can be a challenge to find pastry flour. Even well-stocked supermarkets seldom carry it. If you can't find pastry flour, you can substitute plain flour.

# CONTENTS

## Acknowledgements

# TANYA

Firstly, I need to recognize the most important woman in my life, my stepmother Pat. Without her loving support throughout my entire life I wouldn't be the person I am today. Her guidance, knowledge, and belief in my abilities has been a crucial inspiration. Thanks to the rest of my family, whose support does not go unnoticed: Kari and Trevor, my beloved siblings; Nana and Papa, for loving support; Bob, Jordan, and Stephanie, for being there. Also, a special thank you to all other family members, of whom there are too many to name.

Chris, whose love, patience and wit has helped me in innumerable ways, especially by providing me with renewed energy sources when I was exhausted beyond belief. I need to thank my patient housemates: Tracy, Dylan, and Pat. Thanks for letting me use your computer for endless hours, and keeping me sane. Appreciation to the Benny's crew: Lisa, Mo, and Ben. These three ladies, who I've shared laughter, knowledge, and inspiration with, have greatly enriched my life.

Thanks to the encouraging Dawn crew, especially Sarah T., Lance, and Noah. Your combined wisdom has provided me with essential motivation and insight. I'm grateful to my friend Jamie. His motivation, integrity, and brilliance leave me constantly in awe. Special thanks to my friend Toni, whose help and encouragement has had a significant impact on me and this project.

Special thanks to all whom are far in miles but not in thoughts. Kyla, Dave, JB, all kids from the Springfield era. The Vic West crew. Chris, Jen, and Kieran. Rob and Todd. Gerry. Sivan. Jana at Earth's Herbal. Again, a list that could go on for miles. All of these people have touched and enriched my life in unimaginable ways.

Recognition to the furry and feathered beings without voice: they provide me with inspiration and drive, especially my sweet, lovable cat, Chicken.

I want to acknowledge all the organizations and businesses who stand for social change. These groups are held together by people who selflessly strive for a more humane world. I thank them for being true to their beliefs.

Sarah, my beautiful friend and co-author, whose friendship means the world to me. Without her encouragement and support through all my endeavours, I don't know where I would be. I have the deepest admiration for her strength, wisdom, and brilliance.

Lastly, thanks to Blaine, Brian, Lisa, and everyone at Arsenal Pulp Press. Due to their vision and expertise, they have taken this dream of mine, and made it into a reality.

Acknowledgements

# SARAH

There are so many people I need to thank, without them this book would not have been possible. At the risk of forgetting someone, I need to thank those closest to me by name for their support and guidance: Gerry, for his patience, wisdom, and love. My niece Heidi, for filling my heart with joy. My father Ken, for teaching me by example how to be creative, eccentric, and self-confident, and for giving me the space and guidance to discover who I was in my own time. To my mum Sue, for her love, for being the beginning of everything I am now and for leaving a little piece of her spirit in me before she died.

There are two women who have taught me about grace, beauty, and what it means to be a woman: my stepmum Denise and my Auntie Bonnie. I am so thankful to have them as female role models, and I especially need to thank Denise for sticking by me all these years, even when I was a horrible step daughter. Thanks to my brother Ben for his wisdom in the kitchen and his partner Sarah for her laughter. My cousins Stacy and Natasha, for loving and supporting me no matter what. My Zeyda, Art and his wife Lee, for always pushing me to be a better person. Black Bumps, Riley, Sir Douglas Fort, and Chelvin for teaching me about unconditional love. My Grandma Em for making me cardigans, my Aunt Jean, Uncle Geoff and their family for loving and supporting me from so far away. To Corri for her endless love and support. Thanks to Jen, Kieran and Chris, Maureen, JB, Chris, Jana and Korma, Trinity and Steph, and of course, the one and only Larry. Thanks to Pat, Richard, Matthew, Bertha, and Faye. Thanks to Timm, Greg, and Bubba for their integrity. Thank you to Mike and the Stark Raving Tattoo crew, the Capital City Scooter Club, and Earth's Herbal Products. To Cheryl, Leslie, Vanna, Rebecca, Meagan, Shana, Maury, and Graham. The Deverall, Miller, Howard, Ball, Sperling, Cuddington, and Smollett families. Thank you to the Vic West crew and the Springfield roommates who have all moved away, but are still close to my heart. Thanks to my Regina friends, who knew me at my worst and still like me. And of course to Blaine, Brian, and everyone at Arsenal Pulp for their encouragement and support.

I especially need to thank my co-author Tanya. Through good and bad and even worse, she has consistently been the one person I can count on no matter what happens. Her dedication, beauty and strength leave me breathless. Without her, I honestly don't know where I'd be. Her support, frequent pushing, and love make me a better person and for her I am ever so thankful.

A final thanks to everyone who has been so supportive of us and our endeavour. Without your help, suggestions, recipe ideas, excitement, and smiling faces this book would feel hollow. Thank you very much.

Now quit looking for your name and go make something yummy!

# INTRODUCTION

# HOW WE BOTH VEGAN

We vegan in the early 1990s, when we were both lazy vegetarians who occasionally used and consumed animal products. We decided to make the transition to veganism because of our belief in a simple, but important, value: we love and respect animals and the earth. Once we chose to give up eating all animal products, we discovered, with just a little imagination and some good advice, how easy it was to go vegan.

We all choose veganism for different reasons. Maybe it's a fervent belief in animal rights. Perhaps it's a desire to try a healthier diet. Whatever the reason, you can be vegan and still eat wonderful food. And as this book demonstrates, veganism is not something to be afraid of. There is a popular belief that by removing animal products from one's diet, food will become necessarily boring, a life of dining on grass and shrubs. But let us assure you: vegan food is fabulous food, full of flavour and all the nutrients you need.

In the winter of 1996 we came up with the idea of collecting our vegan recipes in a magazine-style cookbook that we could share with our families and friends. We slaved over the computer, spending countless hours typing and organizing our recipes, putting great love and care into our project. We printed and bound the books ourselves and went about giving them away as gifts and selling them where we could for cost. This little book then began to snowball, selling like vegan hotcakes wherever we went. Then a light bulb went on: Let's go legit! So we shopped for a publisher and the rest is history.

All the old tried-and-true recipes from our first book are here, as well as a bunch of new ones, and some tips and tricks to living vegan. If you're a curious first-timer, we hope this book will ease your transition to the vegan way. And if you're a full-fledged vegan warrior, you'll probably be pleasantly surprised by some recipes you've never tried before.

Being vegan starts with an open mind. Once you've given these recipes a try, we hope you will adapt them to suit your own individual palate. Just add your own imagination and stir!

We've made these recipes relatively simple to prepare. There are just a few things that you should have that will make your life easier:

- A good kitchen environment. Cooking should be a pleasure!

- The correct ingredients. There's nothing worse than discovering you don't have everything you need in the middle of preparing a recipe.

- A food processor. Your food processor is your best friend. If you don't have a food processor, a blender will do. But if you can afford one, it's a tool you will use forever.

- The proper equipment.

**Every kitchen should have:**

food processor or blender
measuring spoons
mixing bowls (small, medium, and large)
mixing spoons
a good knife or two
vegetable peeler
stock pot, saucepans, steamer
baking sheet, loaf tin, 23x33cm/9x13in baking tray, muffin tins, roasting tin
cooling rack
grater
sieve
whisk
potato masher
colander
rolling pin
greaseproof paper
timer
a good imagination!

Remember, your equipment doesn't have to be brand new or expensive; most of the utensils can be found second-hand – reduce, reuse, and recycle! Once you've assembled your ingredients and your utensils, try one recipe at a time – and don't forget to compost!

We'd love to hear from you – check out our website: www.govegan.net for contact details.

So make some tea, get out your apron, and let's get cooking. And always remember – you are what you eat!

**SARAH & TANYA**

## HOW SARAH VEGAN

I have an extraordinarily strong connection to the kitchen – the warmth, the smells, the sounds. No matter whose house I'm in, I always find myself gravitating to this room. I love looking in people's refrigerators, seeing what kind of spices they have, their canned goods, their cooking utensils. A kitchen is a perfect reflection of its owner. You know immediately if they enjoy food, or if they just eat to keep from being hungry. A well-stocked kitchen is a thing of beauty, so if you catch me looking in your cupboards, I'm not snooping . . . I'm just trying to get to know you better.

Why am I vegan? I get that question a lot. My journey into the world of veganism has been a life-long adventure. I was born and raised a vegetarian in Regina, Saskatchewan. My mother believed in the old adage, "You are what you eat," and she raised my little brother and me accordingly. Growing up vegetarian in a prairie town wasn't always easy. There was a tiny health food shop called Ina's that was in the basement of a woman's house. I loved going there to visit; I was intrigued by all the different items and it always smelled so exotic. When my mum died, my father continued to raise us as vegetarians. I recently asked my dad why he didn't start serving us meat after she died, since he has always been a meat lover. He told me that as a little girl I was always sickened by the thought of eating meat. We ate dairy and eggs, but animal flesh didn't touch my lips until I was about thirteen years old.

My friends were always trying to get me to try meat. I think I was the only vegetarian in school and I didn't really have a clear reason as to why. It made me feel like a weirdo, an outcast, but the thought of eating meat made me feel sick to my stomach, which pretty much kept me from experimenting. One summer I was camping with my friend Shana and her family. We ended up getting lost on Jan Lake in the fog and had to spend the night on an island in a lean-to her brother Adam built. The next morning there was nothing to eat but a huge stick of pepperoni. Being super-hungry, I took the plunge. It was my first taste of meat. It wasn't so bad. I actually enjoyed how salty it was, and it didn't look anything like an animal, so I managed to get it down.

As a teenager I dabbled in meat occasionally. My stepmum made a mean almond chicken; when I ate it, I'd close my eyes and pretend that it wasn't meat. Or I'd cram down her burgers before my brain would tell my stomach I was eating dead flesh. But after a few bites, I would have to stop. I think I've always felt that eating animals is wrong.

I moved out of my parents' house at seventeen and was on my own for the first time. I couldn't afford anything but Japanese noodles and ketchup. Back then, my roommate Corri and I would spend all of our money on cigarettes, punk shows, beer, and rent. If there was anything left over, we'd buy some food. It seems insane to me now that food was so low on my list of priorities. For a long time, I had a very strange relationship with food. For example, I couldn't eat vegetables that had veins (such as tomatoes or lettuce) and I had no idea how to cook. I lived off noodles and packaged food for years. The crappy food was part of an even crappier lifestyle, and eventually my health deteriorated.

I moved from Regina to Victoria, B.C. in late 1988. I wanted a fresh start, to reinvent myself a little. I found two cookbooks at a garage sale that my mum used to use, *Laurel's Kitchen* and *Diet For a Small Planet*. Slowly I learned how to cook the foods my mum used to make me. I began to really enjoy spending time in the kitchen. I would bake bread every Sunday; while sitting in the quiet of my kitchen waiting for my bread to rise, I would write letters and hang out with my cats. The time I spent in that kitchen on Bay Street was amazing. It was a metamorphosis of sorts. I started buying more cookbooks, became interested in environmental issues, and started stepping away from conventional cleaners and products that were tested on animals.

I would still occasionally dabble in bacon and sandwich meat. Mostly because I'm a saltaholic, and the fact that these products didn't look like anything that used to be alive. It wasn't until I got my first pet that my ideals and beliefs started to really form. I never had a pet growing up (except for a couple of guppies that I accidentally killed and two gerbils who I'm convinced committed suicide). I received Chelvin the cat as a birthday present and soon his brother Black Bumps came to live with us as well. We moved to a new house and with the house came another cat, Riley. After Riley came Sir Douglas Fort. These cats and my experience with them has changed my life forever. They aren't pets to me anymore; they are part of my family and have taught me more about animals and their rights to a happy life than any book, movie, or conversation ever has.

My appreciation of animals and their emotions has made me a better person. Some people may want to call it anthropomorphism; I call it a wake-up call. When Chelvin died, his brother B.B. was devastated. He would circle the spot where Chelvin's body had been, and would lay in my bed and cry; he wouldn't eat for over a week. It broke my heart. It was then that I realized that these fuzzy little creatures feel emotions like we do.

At the same time my health began to deteriorate. I was still a vegetarian and I believed strongly in animal rights, but was still wearing leather and eating dairy and eggs. I became so ill I couldn't work, could barely function, and was bedridden for over a month. Finally, after seeing more than ten doctors and enduring numerous horrible tests, I was finally diagnosed with chronic fatigue syndrome (CFS). I was so weak I could barely feed myself, and relied heavily on my friends for help. I started reading every book on CFS I could and decided that a vegan life-style would be the best for me. I got allergy tests, and cut out all sugars, caffeine, alcohol, and animal products.

I started paying attention to my body. Listening to what it needed. When I'm tired, I rest. When I'm hungry, I eat. My health is not yet up to 100 per cent, but I'm getting close. When I think back to how sick I was eight years ago, and the strides I have made in my lifestyle, I am so thankful for all of the support from my friends and family. I think my illness is symptomatic of what happens to a lot of people: we spend too much time ignoring our bodies and pushing ourselves to do more than we are capable of. Our culture teaches us that it is okay to overload on chemicals and waste. We slowly poison ourselves, and eventually our bodies give up.

So... why vegan? Out of respect for my mum, my cats, and myself. To be healthy again, and to encourage my family, friends, and community to be healthy, too. I also feel that, for me, using and consuming animal products is wrong. This is my choice, my journey. I am choosing to be the best person I can be, and for me it starts with living vegan and being as environmentally responsible as I can.

There are so many events that have brought me to this point. One of them is my best friend Tanya. Through the nine-plus years that we've been friends, we've somehow seemed to be always on the same page. We've lost friends, and made new ones; we've lived together, lived in different cities, and lived through many demented experiences together. While there have been many changes in my life, the one constant has been Tanya. She took care of me when I was sick, held my hand when I've been scared, and stood side by side with me while we cooked. I couldn't ask for a better friend.

This book reveals just part of what I enjoy about living vegan. I hope that with this book, you will discover how to use your imagination when it comes to cooking and eating – to open your mind, to listen to your tastebuds, and to share what you learn with your loved ones. Food, friends, and family: there is nothing I like better! **Sarah**

## How Tanya Vegan

I grew up in a household where it was believed that "meat is the fuel that keeps bodies healthy and strong." My father was an adamant meat-eater; he loved the stuff. Throughout my formative years, he would always say to me, "We have to eat at least two servings of meat daily." I never questioned this; I had no reason to because I didn't know any different.

Once when I was eleven, I remember going out for burgers with my family and being disgusted with the amount of vegetables piled on top of my all-beef patty. "If I wanted a salad, I would have ordered one," I said to my fellow diners. They all laughed. Meat – I used to love the stuff.

It wasn't until years later that I began to cultivate my own ideas and beliefs surrounding food. Leasa, my best friend in high school, introduced me to the idea of vegetarianism. She had come back from a family vacation to California, and while driving along the beautiful California coastline, they had passed by a slaughterhouse. The stench emanating from it disgusted her so much that she refrained from eating animals from that day forward. Her passion and convictions intrigued me, but while I was interested in her ideas, I still thought in order to be healthy, I had to eat meat at least twice daily.

Leasa and I moved into our first apartment together after finishing high school. Our interests at the time were in punk rock shows and booze, which is what we spent most of our money on. We bought food from our local 7-11, and ate out in restaurants a lot. We didn't care what we ate, just as long as it was cheap and plentiful. Meat started to become less and less important to me, and after a while, I gave up eating meat for good. That's when I started to call myself a vegetarian.

I maintained my vegetarian lifestyle for about five years until I decided that veganism was the path for me. This transition didn't take place overnight; it was definitely a slow process. I refrained from calling myself an outright vegan for a while, until I was sure I had made the right decision. Turning vegan was a much harder transition than becoming vegetarian because there were so many unanswered questions. For example, if I didn't drink milk, where would I get my calcium? And what about iron and protein? Not only that, but I also had to convince my family and friends that my new lifestyle was a healthy one, and that I wouldn't suffer for my choices.

Luckily, I have Sarah. We were sharing a house with some other people during the period when we both decided, at around the same time, to take the plunge into veganism. We were able to adhere to one another's concerns about our lifestyle changes. This made my transition a lot smoother. Through her wisdom and strength, I was able to keep true to my beliefs no matter how hard it seemed.

Now, I believe my decision to go vegan is one of the best I've ever made. I also believe that in order for this planet to survive, we need to take a good look at what we eat and how we act – not only what we put into our mouths, but also what we put on our bodies, what we clean our houses with, and how we live our lives. Most humans selfishly think that we are detached from the rest of the species on Earth. But in truth, we are all part of an integrated whole: humans, animals, plants, all things living. Our actions, no matter how small or large, can have a tremendous impact on the well-being of humans, animals, and eco-systems. It's your choice if you want your life to have a positive or negative effect on the world.

There was a time when we were able to harvest vegetables from our gardens, eat our own chickens' eggs, drink our own cows' milk, and from these sources nourish our bodies. It was also possible to sustain ourselves by saving and using the seeds that our gardens offered. The sacred act of eating – to maintain our bodies' physical, mental, and spiritual well-being – should be so simple. Instead it has evolved into an exploitative act where factory farming, genetic engineering, and the increasing use of pesticides are now the norm. It is a fact that one of the secrets to our health and happiness is right in front of us on a daily basis: food. It's the fuel that our bodies assimilate and turn into energy. If you are eating food that is unhealthy, you yourself will feel unhealthy. It's that simple.

It saddens me that we live in a culture that obsesses over fat. Food is reduced to how many calories and grams of fat it contains. Healthy lifestyles should begin by making conscious decisions about the food we eat and things we do to make it a better world. But don't let me tell you what to do. Get out and read books and magazines and websites to get the facts. Then cultivate your own ideas and philosophies of how to live life. For me, becoming a vegan was not only a decision to make me feel more healthy and alive, but also to save our planet and all who inhabit it. **Tanya**

# VEGANISM 101

So you've finally decided to take the plunge to go vegan! At first it may seem overwhelming, maybe even frightening. We are here to make your transition a little easier.

A "true vegan" is someone who does not consume or use any animal products. True veganism can be impractical in today's world. Just remember, the goal of the vegan is to get as close to the ideal as possible. This doesn't mean you can cheat and have a fried egg sandwich or a sausage pizza whenever you feel the need to have a "vegan time-out". This means that you must strive each day to remain "true" to your beliefs. We're not here to judge one another, or monitor others' habits; we're just trying to be the best vegans we can be. As the saying goes, "One vegan day at a time."

We will start off with the most basic facet of veganism:

## Food

Food is not just fuel for our bodies. Becoming vegan can open the door to a wonderful culinary journey. Being a lazy vegetarian is easy – just omit the meat, and you're there. Becoming vegan takes a bit more time and energy and a lot more imagination. The first step is always the hardest, but the results are worth it.

### 1. Dairy
Delete, omit, cut it from your diet. It is not necessary. After all, cow's milk is for baby cows! Experiment. Go to your local health food shop and peruse the shelves. There are dozens of dairy substitutes available (soy, rice, barley, etc.). You could also try making some yourself (see the chapter on Milks& Beverages). In the beginning, try spending about a week or so completely dairy-free. Don't cheat by putting milk in your coffee or butter on your toast. After a few days you'll find your sense of taste begins to change. You can slowly introduce your body to one dairy substitute, and then, slowly, to others. By then your tastebuds won't be expecting something that tastes like milk. Alas, omitting dairy also includes removing cheese from your palate. Cheese is a hard one to leave behind, but your colon will thank you.

### 2. Eggs
Once you've deleted all dairy from your diet, it's time to eliminate the eggs. You probably never really liked the slimy things anyway. And what is that weird, cloudy, chewy stuff all about? There are many substitutions (see page 19), one of the best being tofu. Try it scrambled with veggies, spices, or anything else you can think of. (You'll find plenty of tofu ideas beginning on page 39.)

### 3. Meat
It goes without saying that you won't be eating anything that used to be an animal, and that includes fish. They have hearts, eyes, and a brain. They count, too.

## Know What You're Eating

Food labelling can be tricky, and you should get into the habit of checking the ingredients of all prepared foods before you include them in your shopping basket. And remember, buying food can be fun. We're all trying to fit thirty hours into a twenty-four-hour day, and while shopping can be a challenge, it doesn't have to be a chore.

## Go Organic

Organic. What does this word mean to you? Overpriced fruits and vegetables? Incredible tasting food? Not sure? Organic foods are rapidly making their way into the mainstream. These foods offer you the healthiest choice possible while at the same time protecting our environment and the health of our planet. The word "organic" is used to describe food whose growth has not been assisted by the use of chemicals. Most commercial crops are sprayed with a wide array of herbicides, pesticides, fungicides, and rodent killers, with over seventy of these being known carcinogens. After spraying, they remain on or in the food and can present long-term health risks.

Organic farmers work to produce crops without harming the consumer, farm workers, soil, water, wildlife, or the environment. Organic farming methods were the norm prior to the 1940s. Since then, with the arrival of chemical agriculture, there has been a dramatic increase in environmental damage, such as water contamination and topsoil erosion. There has also been an increase in illnesses and cancers in humans. Although organic foods cost a little more than conventional food, the taste alone should convince you to switch. You are worth it! What you consume is the fuel that runs your body. Eating hollow, tasteless foods that have been blanketed by chemicals and injected with dyes can do nothing but lessen the enjoyment and nutritional value of your food.

Organic farming is a growing but relatively small industry that cannot survive without our support. Its practices are often labour intensive and most of the farmers' crops don't even make it to neighbourhood organic markets due to the condition of the produce. Without the help of pesticides and herbicides, it is difficult to obtain what many people consider to be "perfect" looking vegetables.

**5 reasons to go organic:**

1. Organic foods taste better, and may be more nutritious.
2. Organic foods are safer for consumers and farmers.
3. Organic farming protects the environment.
4. Purchasing organic food can help support local farmers.
5. Organic farming works with natural systems rather than seeking to dominate them.

Organic food offers you the healthiest choice possible and protects our environment and the health of our planet. Support local organic farmers and suppliers, or plant your own garden.

## Eating Out

Eating out is always difficult for vegans. There is nothing worse than staring into the face of a waiter who has no clue what vegan means, and having to order just a salad when you had your heart set on a more substantial meal. Choose your restaurants wisely. Phone ahead and ask if they can accommodate you. That way, you'll narrow down your options and you won't have to leave starving and grumpy. Carry a card with a list of the foods you won't eat. Tell your waiter that you are "allergic" to the items listed and ask them to inform the chef. It may be a tiny lie to tell them that you're allergic, but allergies make restaurants stop and listen. Just make sure to thank them for providing special service. A nice tip is a good way, too.

If we're travelling and don't know the town well, the first thing we do is phone the local health food shop to ask for places to eat. If there is no such shop, we stick to ethnic foods. Asian, Middle Eastern, and Mexican foods can usually accommodate a hungry vegan. Having said all of this, most of the vegans we know prefer to eat at home. You know what you're eating and there is no chance of a mistake.

## If Mum Gets Worried

If your family gets worried that you're not getting enough nutrients by becoming vegan, tell them they don't need to. If you're eating a well-balanced, well-planned meal, you're probably getting all the things you need to stay healthy and happy. If you're concerned about your diet, please consult a nutritionist who is well versed in veganism. They can help to guide you in your food planning. But remember, finding a nutritionist, much like a doctor or any other service, is like finding a pair of shoes. You have to try a few on before you find the one you like.

Here's a brief list of foods, from the book *Prescription for Nutritional Healing* by James and Phyllis Balch, that have some of the nutrients and vitamins we need to include in our diet.

**Protein:** It has been suggested that we need about 50 grams of protein per day. To make a complete protein, combine beans with brown rice, sweetcorn, nuts, seeds, or wheat. Or combine brown rice with beans, nuts, seeds, or wheat. Also, soybean products are complete proteins. Consult a nutritionist if you have any concerns about your protein intake.

**Calcium:** Calcium is found in green, leafy vegetables. Other food sources include almonds, asparagus, black strap molasses, brewer's yeast, broccoli, cabbage, carob, spring greens, dandelion greens, dulse (a sea vegetable), figs, kale, kelp, mustard greens, and watercress. Herbs that contain calcium include alfalfa, burdock root, cayenne pepper, chamomile, chickweed, chicory, dandelion, fennel seed, flaxseed, kelp, nettle, paprika, parsley, peppermint, plantain, and many more. Consult a nutritionist if you have any concerns about your calcium intake.

**Iron:** Iron is found in green leafy vegetables, whole grains, almonds, avocados, beetroot, blackstrap molasses, brewer's yeast, dates, dulse, kelp, kidney and butter beans, millet, peaches, pears, prunes, pumpkins, raisins, rice and wheat bran, sesame seeds, soybeans, and watercress. Herbs that contain iron include alfalfa, catnip, cayenne pepper, chamomile, chickweed, dandelion, fennel seed, kelp, lemongrass, paprika, parsley, peppermint, plantain and many more. Consult a nutritionist if you have any concerns about your iron intake.

B12: There are large amounts of B12 found in brewer's yeast. Sea vegetables such as dulse, kelp, and nori are also high in B12, as are soybean and soy products. Consult a nutritionist if you have any concerns about your B12 intake.

## You Are What You Wear

Veganism encompasses so much more than food, and now that you have mastered the basics of eating, it is time to update your wardrobe. There are many shops and companies who sell vegan clothing. Support and reward local shops who carry vegan clothing.

Thinking about your clothing means every article: shoes, belts, jackets, sweaters. There is nothing worse than expressing your vegan beliefs to someone who then points out your dead cow shoes. Leather is everywhere: the label on your jeans, the collar on your jacket, the watchstrap on your wrist. And don't forget about wool and silk; they're animal products, too. If you choose to remove all animal products from your wardrobe, please donate them to a charity store or shelter. Remember: reduce, reuse, and recycle. This is where personal choice comes into play.

## The Vegan Police

Becoming vegan doesn't mean you are suddenly the vegan police, so don't judge others or try to catch them doing something un-vegan. Pay attention to your own life. What kind of vegan do you want to be? Will you subscribe only to the belief that our animal friends shouldn't be eaten? Will you remove all things from your life that contain animal products? Will you reduce, reuse, and recycle everything you can so that this planet is a clean, healthy place for animals and people? We both wear leather shoes. That's because we're not just pro-animal, we're also pro-Earth. It's our belief that nothing should be wasted. We will never buy new leather products again, but will continue to use the ones we bought before we went vegan. Sarah has had the same leather belt for over eight years, and it will probably last another eight. She wants to use up her possessions rather than send them to landfill so that she can buy an animal-friendly replacement. When the time comes for a new belt, she'll opt for the vegan one. That's our personal choice. Our decision to make. What's yours?

## Home Is Where the Heart Is

Don't forget about your house. Look around. Is your furniture made from leather? Will you find wool blankets and feather pillows on the bed, animal-tested cleaners and chemicals under the sink?

What about your toothpaste, your beauty products? How far are you willing to go? You can follow a few simple steps that just require a little time. Read your labels and support animal-friendly products, companies, and shops. Veganism is an easy choice; everything about it suggests a positive and productive lifestyle.

## Educate Yourself

Read a book, talk to people, figure out what you believe. Your local library and the internet both have a huge source of vegan information that you may or may not agree with. Read it all and decide for yourself. There are many ways to make your life animal friendly. Reading labels is a good way to start. People for the Ethical Treatment of Animals (PETA) at **www.peta.org.uk** produce a list of animal-product ingredients to avoid and companies that test or use animal products.

You can join the Vegan Society and you may even have a local branch. They are the best source of all information relating to an animal-free lifestyle. They produce a very handy guide the *Animal Free Shopper*. Contact them for a free information pack at Donald Watson House, 21 Hylton Street, Hockley, Birmingham B18 6HJ , tel: 0845 458 8244 or  +44 121 523 1730, email: info@vegansociety.com and go to their website **www.vegansociety.com**

## Ideas to Bring Food, Family, Friends, and Fun Together!

- Host a vegan supper in which everyone picks a recipe and brings it to the party. Make sure everyone doesn't pick salad!
- Host a vegan supper-style birthday party: the best way to celebrate life.
- Make a dish for a friend: if a friend is laid up, just had a baby, or down in the dumps, make them something to eat. Share your favourite recipe and pass on your love and your love of food.
- Make vegan food for a charitable organization. Share the wealth!
- Visit your grandma or someone in a nursing home and bring some vegan cookies.

# ALTERNATIVES & SUBSTITUTIONS

Vegan versions of foods traditionally made with animal products are great not only for vegans, but for those who suffer from food allergies as well. Here is a list of vegan substitutes for eggs, peanut butter, and milk, as well as lists for variations on staples such as flour and sugar. There are also hints for that great mother of all food substitutes, tofu. Going vegan or having allergies can be a challenge; again, imagination is the key.

# EGGS

The following are some healthy alternatives to high-cholesterol eggs. Each of these substitutions has a distinct flavour and method of use. Experiment with them all when cooking and baking to see how they can be used. Each one is the equivalent of 1 egg unless otherwise noted:

- Flax eggs (3 tablespoons = 1 egg) (pg. 151)
  Flax is great for pancakes, breads, and other baking.
- 1½ teaspoons powder egg replacer plus 2 tablespoons water
  Most health food shops carry egg replacer.
- 1/2 banana
  Bananas are great egg substitutes for desserts, or sweet items like pancakes or smoothies.
- 25g/1oz tofu
  When using tofu as an egg substitute, ensure you're using soft tofu, and a food processor, so you don't get any grainy bits.
- 3 tablespoons apple sauce
  Like bananas, apple sauce is great for sweeter recipes.
- 1 tablespoon psyllium husks plus 2 tablespoons water
  The longer you let the psyllium husks sit in water, the more they become an eggy substance. Terrific in breads and baking.

# MILK

Humans consume cow's milk as a beverage but it was designed for baby cows, not humans. There are so many milk substitutes out there on the market, and each brand has its own taste. Try them all and find the ones you like best, or better yet, try making your own.

- Soy milk (pg. 27)
- Rice milk (pg. 28)
- Oatmeal milk (pg. 28)
- Coconut milk (pg. 29)

# BUTTER

Butter is made from churning whole milk or cream until the fats separate and form a solid mass. It has a high salt and saturated fat content and is thought to contribute to heart disease. These substitutions offered are not only nutritious, but taste great in baking, too.

- Vegan butter (pg. 80)
- Soy lecithin spread
- Shop-bought margarine (check the label for animal products – see Appendix for list)
- Flax oil  - don't use this for baking or cooking, but as a topping for potatoes, rice, popcorn, etc.
- Nut butter  - can be made from almonds, cashews, or other nuts.
- Vegetable shortening  - use for making pastry.
- Apple sauce  - use for baking only; can replace up to 3/4 of butter in a recipe.

# CHEESE

There are hundreds of varieties of cheeses offered throughout the world. Sadly, only a few varieties of "mock" cheeses made from rice or soy are available; sadder still, even fewer brands offer vegan versions. (Some brands contain casein, which is an animal by-product.) Check the ingredients before buying your mock cheese, which is available in most health food shops.

- Soy, rice cheese
- Soy, rice Parmesan cheese
- Faux Parmesan Cheese (pg. 154)

# PEANUT BUTTER

Peanut butter is the most familiar and common nut butter around. But many people are severely allergic to peanuts. It is possible to enjoy the same rich flavouring as peanuts by substituting any of the seed butters located in the list below. Different nuts and seed butters have different tastes, so experiment with them all and choose your favourite. Here are a few examples available in most health food shops.

- Tahini (sesame seed)
- Almond butter
- Cashew butter
- Sunflower seed butter

# SUGAR

Here are a few examples of natural alternatives to those white and brown granules found in most homes. Generally found in most health food shops, these alternatives offer a more holistic and healthy approach to sweetening your foodstuffs. Remember that when using a liquid sweetener, you must cut back a little on the other liquid in the recipe.

- Maple syrup
- Cane sugar
- Date sugar
- Barley malt
- Fruit juice concentrate

# FLOUR

Wheat is a very popular grain and is used to make bread products, as a thickening agent – the list goes on and on. Your local health food shop probably offers a number of grains that can be used in place of wheat, each one having a different flavour and density. Try them all. In addition to these different kinds of flour, you can make your own in a blender or a food processor. For example, you can make oat flour by blending rolled oat flakes until powdered.

- **Spelt flour:** Tends to make your recipes heavier; you can slightly increase the baking powder so that it rises more. Good for bread and baking.
- **Kamut flour:** Good for bread and other baking; best if used half and half with other flours.
- **Barley flour:** Good for pancakes, cookies.
- **Buckwheat flour:** Good for pancakes, but is a heavy flour so use half and half with other flours.
- **Oat flour:** Good for breads, cookies.
- **Brown rice flour**
- **Cornflour**
- **Millet flour:** A dry, coarse flour.
- **Potato flour**
- **Soy flour:** Has a strong flavour.
- **Chickpea flour:** Has a strong flavour.

# OIL

Oil is an essential part of the daily diet, needed for a variety of purposes to keep the body healthy and strong. Generally, oils are used in baking, cooking, or as a topping on rice or salad. Try to use organic cold-pressed oil, which can be found in most health food shops.

- **Olive Oil:** The best oil there is. Splurge a little, because it's worth it! We even use it in our baking, but it does have a distinct flavour, so you may want to use sunflower oil when you bake.
- **Sunflower oil, safflower oil, canola oil, vegetable oil:** These are cheaper oils that can be used for basically anything.
- **Sesame oil:** Has a strong taste; not good for frying. Excellent oil for salads and Asian recipes.
- **Flax oil:** Don't cook with this oil! Use it for salads, or in place of butter on popcorn, potatoes, and rice.

# SALT

Increasing levels of salt in our diets in the last few decades have led to wide concern. Salt finds its way into our lives by means of flavour enhancers and food preservatives. Instead of reaching for the salt shaker, replace it with these nutritious substitutions.

- **Gomashio** (pg. 154): A condiment made of roasted sesame seeds. Use on cooked vegetables, salads, soups.
- **Braggs:** Braggs, an all-purpose seasoning brand, is formulated vegetable protein made from pure soybeans and purified water. Great on salads and dressings, soups, veggies, rice and beans, tofu, stir-fries, tempeh, casseroles, potatoes, vegan jerky, popcorn, gravies, and sauces.

# TOFU

Tofu is a white, semi-solid product made from soy milk and a curdling agent. Tofu by itself is almost tasteless. It can be used as a filler or substitution or on its own. Think of tofu as a sponge: it will soak up whatever it's surrounded by. Tofu is high in protein and calcium, low in fat and sodium, and cholesterol-free.

There are many kinds of tofu. Which one to use depends on your recipe:

- **Firm:** Good for stir-fries, scrambled tofu, tofu jerky.
- **Medium:** Easily blended; good for stir-fries, scrambled tofu, tofu jerky, sauces, desserts.
- **Soft and silken:** Very easily blended; good for desserts, dips, sauces.

## Buying Tofu

When you buy tofu, choose one that has the same consistency as the recipe requires or the ingredient you are replacing. Buying tofu is like buying wine: each brand has a different texture, a different taste. Shop around until you find the one you like.

## Drain Your Tofu

Before using your tofu, place it in a colander over the sink. Let it sit for 5 to 10 minutes so excess water may drain out. You can help it along by giving it a loving squeeze! Note: use this method carefully when working with soft and silken tofu.

## Storing Tofu

Store your tofu in an air-tight container. Fill the container with water until the tofu is covered. If you are using only part of a package of tofu, recover the remainder with fresh water daily. An open package of tofu will last 4-6 days if stored properly. If it starts to smell "beany" or the water becomes cloudy, then it's time to compost it.

## Freezing Tofu

Freezing tofu will give it a chewy, meaty texture. First, open the tofu package, drain well, and press out any excess water. Seal it in a plastic bag and freeze for at least 8 hours. To thaw quickly, pour hot water over the tofu, then press excess water out before using.

## Tempeh

A somewhat meat-like substance made from cultured soybeans. It is used in dishes like chicken salad (pg. 63) or in barbecuing, and has a rather strong taste compared to tofu.

# TVP OR TEXTURED VEGETABLE PROTEIN

A soy product that comes in granules or chunks. Rehydrate it in water following the packet instructions and use in place of minced meat as in chilli. It takes on the flavour (somewhat) of whatever you cook it with.

# MISO

Made from fermented soybeans, and usually is found in a paste form. It is used as a flavouring agent and for soup stocks and gravies. There are 3 basic varieties of miso: soybean, barley, and brown rice; each has a different and distinct flavour and colour. Look for this in Japanese food markets or health food shops. Hint: add only at the end of cooking; boiling it will ruin its properties.

# BEANS

Although there are hundreds of varieties of beans available throughout the world – each one having a unique history and place of origin – only about 10 to 15 varieties are commonly used. Be imaginative and try out different kinds of beans; experiment with different tastes and textures. Beans contain virtually no cholesterol, little fat, and valuable vitamins and minerals. They provide necessary protein and are a great source of carbohydrates.

Dry beans should be pre-soaked in a bowl or jar of water in the refrigerator overnight before using; this shortens the cooking time and helps the body to digest them. Make sure to rinse the beans before and after soaking, and discard any flawed beans, such as those with a lighter colour, or any that contain insect punctures.

Here is a list of readily available beans, and their suggested cooking times:

- **Adzuki beans:** Combine 175g/6oz of pre-soaked beans with 1 litre/1$3/4$ pints of water, bring to a boil, then simmer on medium heat for 1-1$1/2$ hours. Stir occasionally.
- **Black beans:** Combine 175g/6oz of pre-soaked beans with 1 litre/1$3/4$ pints of water, bring to a boil, then simmer on medium heat for 1$1/2$-2 hours. Stir occasionally.
- **Chickpeas:** Combine 175g/6oz of pre-soaked beans with 1 litre/1$3/4$ pints of water, bring to a boil, then simmer on medium heat for 1$1/2$-2 hours. Stir occasionally.
- **Kidney beans:** Combine 175g/6oz of pre-soaked beans with 750ml/1$1/4$ pints of water, bring to a boil, then simmer on medium heat for 1$1/4$-1$3/4$ hours. Stir occasionally.
- **Pinto beans:** Combine 175g/6oz of pre-soaked beans with 750ml/1$1/4$ pints of water, bring to a boil, then simmer on medium heat for 1$3/4$-2 hours. Stir occasionally.
- **Haricot beans:** Combine 175g/6oz of pre-soaked beans with 475ml/16fl oz of water, bring to a boil, then simmer on medium heat for 1$1/2$-2 hours. Stir occasionally.
- **Soy beans:** Combine 175g/6oz of pre-soaked beans with 1 litre/1$3/4$ pints of water, bring to a boil, then simmer on medium heat for 3 hours. Stir occasionally.
- **Green and brown lentils:** Combine 225g/8oz of dry lentils with 750ml/1$1/4$ pints of water, bring to a boil, then simmer on medium heat for 25-35 minutes. Stir occasionally.
- **Mung beans:** Combine 175g/6oz of dry beans with 750ml/1$1/4$ pints of water, bring to a boil, then simmer on medium heat for 35-45 minutes. Stir occasionally.
- **Split peas:** Combine 175g/6oz of dry beans with 850ml/28fl oz of water, bring to a boil, then simmer on medium heat for 35-45 minutes. Stir occasionally.

# VEGAN MILKS & BEVERAGES

# MILKS

Really now, what other mammal drinks another species' milk? Only humans carry out this activity. Cow's milk is for baby cows, not for us. Try "milks" made from beans, grains, and nuts. Most supermarkets now carry dairy alternatives. But here are some recipes to try at home.

# FRESH MAPLE VANILLA SOY MILK

There is nothing more delicious than a fresh batch of homemade soy milk. The soybean has its origins in China. One of the world's most versatile beans, it is used to make countless items such as faux meats, tofu, tempeh, miso, and soy sauce. Soybeans contain eight amino acids, and they are very high in vitamin B, protein, and calcium. Soybeans are also a fabulous source of lecithin, which is typically known as brain food. This recipe is a little time consuming...but soooo worth it!

250g/9oz dried soybeans
water

1 tablespoon vanilla extract
3-6 tablespoons maple syrup

In a large bowl, cover the soybeans in 1.5 litres/2 1/2 pints of water. Make sure they are submerged completely. Set aside and leave to soak overnight. When beans have finished soaking (about 8-10 hours), drain out excess water.

In a kettle or small pan, bring 750ml/1 1/4 pints of water to a boil.

In a blender or food processor, blend one-third of the beans with 250ml/8fl oz of boiling water until puréed. Pour into a large stock pot and set aside. Repeat twice with the remaining two-thirds of the beans and add to stock pot.

Add 1.75 litres/3 pints of cold water to the bean purée and slowly bring the mixture to a boil on medium heat, stirring continuously. Once boiled, remove from heat immediately, cover with lid, and set aside to cool.

Once cool enough to handle safely, strain the mixture through a muslin or a metal sieve into a pan. Discard the pulp. Add the vanilla and syrup to the milk and cook for 30 minutes on medium heat, stirring occasionally, in a double boiler. (If you don't have a double boiler, you can use two different-sized pans. Put the milk in the smaller pan and water in the larger one.) Transfer into a jug or container and refrigerate. Stays fresh for 5-7 days. **Makes 1.5 litres/2 1/2 pints.**

# EASY BREEZY RICE MILK

When I lived in Japan I would walk in the countryside and was always amazed at the resourcefulness demonstrated by many of the people there. Open spaces were continuously being transformed into flourishing rice fields. Rice is a staple food for one-half of the world's population. Use brown rice in this recipe if you can, as it contains the most amount of nutrients of all the different varieties of rice. **T**

350g/12oz cooked rice
475ml/16fl oz hot water

maple syrup (to taste)
vanilla extract (to taste)

In a blender or food processor, blend all the ingredients until smooth. This will be quite thick and gets thicker as it sets. Thin the mixture with more water if necessary. Strain any lumps and chill. In addition to drinking it as it is, it may be used in gravies, sauces, and soups in place of milk. **Makes 475ml/16fl oz.**

# AMAZING ALMOND MILK

Almond nuts are high in protein, calcium, and good fats, and they help to eliminate bad fats and cholesterol. When making this milk, try to use organic raw nuts, and you will have the most delicious and nutritious milk money can buy.

60g/2¹/₂oz almonds
475ml/16fl oz water
2 dates, pitted

In a blender or food processor, blend raw almonds until they become a coarse powder. Add water and dates and blend again. Strain any lumps and chill. Good for cereal or porridge. **Makes 475ml/16fl oz.**

# OUTRIGHT OATMEAL MILK

Whether in a nutritious breakfast porridge, a tasty flour, or a milk, the oat is a versatile grain. Use oatmeal milk in gravies, sauces, and soups as a healthy thickening agent instead of cornflour and wheat. Oats contain gluten but are a great alternative to wheat.

1 banana
115g/4oz cooked oatmeal

475ml/16fl oz water
1 teaspoon vanilla extract (optional)

In a blender or food processor, purée all the ingredients until smooth. Place in container with a tight lid and refrigerate. It will keep approximately 4-6 days. **Makes 475ml/16fl oz.**

# CREAMY COCONUT MILK

It has been suggested that coconut is a good source of saturated fat, something that is necessary and poses no threat in a vegan diet. Use this sweet-tasting milk to thicken soups and curries.

250ml/8fl oz boiling water
40g/1½oz desiccated coconut

In a blender or food processor, purée the water and coconut until well incorporated. Strain out coconut bits and chill. **Makes 250ml/8fl oz.**

# SMOOTHIES AND SHAKES

Smoothies and shakes can be made easily and quickly with a bit of imagination and a brave heart. They are great as healthy energy boosters first thing in the morning when you feel like something light, and also midday when you need that extra boost. Bananas are great for their detoxifying qualities.

**Tip: when your bananas start to go spotty and yucky, just peel them, cut them in half, and place them in a plastic bag with a good seal. Throw them in the freezer and when you need them for a smoothie, they will be waiting for you.**

Here are a few smoothie combos to jump-start your imagination and get your mouth watering. The possibilities are endless.

# "ANYTHING GOES" VERY BERRY SHAKE

Enjoy double-fruit flavour in this delicious shake. Spirulina is a microalgae high in protein, vitamin B12, and iron. You can get it in health food or vitamin shops.

475ml/16fl oz soy milk
175g/6oz fresh or frozen berries of your choice

1 frozen banana
1 tablespoon spirulina

In a blender or food processor, purée all the ingredients until smooth. **Makes 2-4 servings.**

# BANANA DATE SHAKE

A sweet, smooth surprise.

350ml/12fl oz soy milk
6 large dates, pitted
2 frozen bananas

In a blender or food processor, purée all the ingredients until thick and creamy. If you like a thinner shake, use 120-175ml/4-6fl oz more milk. **Makes 2 servings.**

# HUKI-LA SMOOTHIE

"Oh, we're going, to a Huki-la!" For fun, serve in a coconut and garnish with pineapple and a paper umbrella. This recipe is also great frozen. Pour into lolly moulds and eat on a hot summer day!

2-4 ice cubes
225g/8oz soft or silken tofu
4-6 strawberries
250ml/8fl oz guava or tropical fruit juice

1 frozen banana
125ml/4fl oz pineapple or apple juice
1oz/25g pineapple (optional)

In a blender or food processor, purée all the ingredients until creamy. **Makes 2-4 servings.**

# TANGY CITRUS SHAKE

A delightful tropical favourite.

1 frozen banana
250ml/8fl oz orange juice
2 tablespoons fresh lime juice

115g/4oz soft or silken tofu
1 teaspoon maple syrup

In a blender or food processor, purée all the ingredients until smooth. Serve and garnish with a slice of lime. **Makes 2 servings.**

# FRESH 'N FRUITY ENERGY SMOOTHIE

You can get soy lecithin and spirulina in health food shops.

350ml/12fl oz apple juice
1 frozen banana
50g/2oz fresh or frozen blueberries

1 heaped teaspoon spirulina
1 heaped teaspoon soy lecithin

In a blender or food processor, purée all the ingredients until smooth and creamy.
**Makes 2-4 servings.**

# IN A HURRY ENERGY SHAKE

Gulp this down and get the hell outta the house.

250ml/8fl oz apple juice
1 teaspoon spirulina

Pour ingredients in a large glass and stir. **Makes 1 serving.**

# BAN-INI

Tahini not only enhances this creamy masterpiece with a unique flavour, but adds
a nutritional element, too.

350ml/12fl oz soy milk
2 frozen bananas
3 tablespoons tahini

2 tablespoons sweetener
1 teaspoon vanilla extract

In a blender or food processor, purée all the ingredients until smooth and creamy.
**Makes 2 servings.**

# TEAS

For centuries teas have been used as a gentle cure for the body's ailments, all the while providing soothing and cosy moments in time. There are hundreds of medicinal herbs that can be used as a daily tonic or for simple pleasure: peppermint for digestion, ginger for fever and nausea, chamomile for relaxation. Many herbs can be grown right outside in your backyard; consult your local herbalist for ideas. The recipes included here are just some ideas of what you can enjoy.

## CURE-ALL GINGER TEA

A healthy hot tea that doesn't make you drowsy. Drink when you feel under the weather.

750ml/1¼ pints water

3 tablespoons or more fresh ginger, peeled and grated

1/8 teaspoon cayenne pepper

sweetener to taste

In a medium saucepan on high heat, bring the water to a boil. Add the ginger and cayenne pepper and reduce heat. Simmer for 20 minutes and strain. Add sweetener to taste. Drink and be healthy. **Makes 2–4 servings.**

## JANA'S EARTH'S HERBAL SUN TEA

This is a nice relaxing tea to drink at the end of the day. Also great for children before bedtime.

1 teaspoon each of fresh or dried: lavender, peppermint, rose, lemon balm

475ml/16fl oz water

In the morning, place herbs in a screw-top glass jar. Add water and cap tightly. Set out in the sun in a nice warm spot, and let steep for the entire day. Once the sun goes down, strain and serve. **Makes 2 servings.**

## JANA'S EARTH'S HERBAL MOON TEA

A lovely longevity tonic.

1 teaspoon each of fresh or dried: raspberry leaf, hawthorn berries, chickweed, calendula flowers

475ml/16fl oz water

In the evening, place ingredients in a screw-top glass jar. Add water but do not cap.
Set jar outside right under the moonlight all night long. Strain and drink first thing in the morning. **Makes 2 servings.**

# SPICED CHAI TEA

A rich, warm tea spiced to perfection. This recipe is also yummy served chilled.

1.5-2 litres/2¹/₂-3¹/₂ pints water
1 tablespoon dried cardamom
1 tablespoon fresh ginger, chopped
¹/₄ teaspoon whole cloves
1 teaspoon black peppercorns

1 cinnamon stick
4 tea bags (orange pekoe or peppermint)
sweetener (to taste)
soy milk (to taste)

In a medium saucepan on high heat, add water, cardamom, ginger, cloves, peppercorns, and cinnamon stick and bring to a boil. Immediately reduce heat and simmer for 5 minutes. Remove from heat and add tea bags. Cover pot and let steep for 5-10 minutes. Strain out into a teapot. Add sweetener and milk to taste. **Makes 2-4 servings.**

# QUICK THAI TEA FOR TWO

A delicious and quick version of the popular tea enjoyed in Thailand.

475ml/16fl oz water
¹/₂ teaspoon dried cardamom
2-4 tablespoons sweetener

125ml/4fl oz soy milk
2 tea bags (orange pekoe or peppermint)

In a small saucepan, add water, cardamom, sweetener, and milk and bring to a boil. Remove from heat and add tea bags. Let steep 3-10 minutes before serving. **Makes 2 servings.**

# QUICK THAI ICED TEA

Sit back, and chill out!

1.5 litres/2¹/₂ pints
1¹/₂ teaspoon dried cardamom
120-175ml/4-6fl oz sweetener

350ml/12fl oz soy milk
4-5 tea bags (orange pekoe or peppermint)
mint sprig (garnish)

In a medium saucepan, add water, cardamom, sweetener, and milk and bring to a boil. Remove from heat and add tea bags. Let steep 3-10 minutes. Remove tea bags and pour into jug and chill for 30-60 minutes. Pour tea over ice in large glasses and serve with a sprig of mint. **Makes 2-4 servings.**

# SAVOURY MISO DRINK

This is a delicious and nutritious alternative to coffee or as a pick-me-up if you're feeling spent. Miso, which you can find in most grocery shops or in health food shops, is rich in both vitamin A and B12.

1 tablespoon miso (light or dark)
1 mug boiling water

Mix ingredients in a mug until miso dissolves. Drink up! **Makes 1 serving.**

# APPLE CIDER HEALTH DRINK

In 400 B.C. Hippocrates, the Father of Medicine, treated his patients with natural cider vinegar for its powerful cleansing, healing, and germ-fighting qualities.

1/2 fresh lemon, sliced
1 tablespoon cider vinegar
1-2 teaspoons liquid sweetener

1/4 teaspoon cayenne pepper
475ml/16fl oz water

In a small saucepan, add all the ingredients and bring to a slow boil over medium heat. Simmer for 5 minutes. Strain and serve. **Makes 1 serving.**

# EGGLESS EGGNOG

Are you a sad vegan warrior whenever the festive season comes around? Feel outta place with no eggnog in hand? Not a problem. Get out your blender and whip up the best eggless nog on the block. After a couple of spiked glasses, no one will be able to tell the difference.

500g/1 1/4 lb silken tofu
475ml/16fl oz soy milk
1 tablespoon vanilla extract
90-150g/3 1/2-5oz dry sweetener

2 tablespoons maple syrup
1/4 teaspoon turmeric
1/4-1/2 teaspoon nutmeg
120-250ml/4-8fl oz rum or brandy (optional)

In a blender or food processor, purée all the ingredients thoroughly until smooth and creamy. Serve well chilled. **Makes 2-4 servings.**

# FIZZY DRINKS

Enjoy making these refreshing drinks as an alternative to shop-bought. Surprisingly easy to make, they add just the right amount of sparkle to tickle your tastebuds.

# FRESH FRUIT JUICE SPRITZER

Light and lively, you can enjoy this any time of the day.

125ml/4fl oz fresh fruit juice of your choice
125ml/4fl oz sparkling mineral water
fruit garnish

Stir the juice and water together in a frosty glass. Serve with a fruit garnish. **Makes 1 serving.**

# SPARKLING HOMEMADE GINGER ALE

Begin festivities with this perky ale.

750ml/1 1/4 pints sparkling mineral water
65g/2 1/2 oz fresh ginger, grated
2-4 tablespoons sweetener (to taste)
cinnamon stick (optional)

Mix all ingredients together in a screw-top glass jar. (In order to avoid having to strain the ginger ale later, you can place the grated ginger in a "tea ball".) Cap tightly and let it steep in the fridge for about half an hour or more. Strain out ginger and serve with a cinnamon stick if desired. **Makes 2 servings.**

# JUICES

A vegetable or fruit juicer is a great kitchen investment. There is nothing finer than a glass of freshly squeezed juice. It's best to drink immediately after making, so you don't lose any vitamins or nutrients. Here are a few great recipes to get your juices running.

## CARROT APPLE GINGER JUICE

Simply the world's greatest juice combination. It tastes great and is nutritious at the same time.

8 carrots, peeled and cut into large chunks
4 apples, peeled, cored, and cut into chunks
5cm/2in piece fresh ginger

Run all the ingredients through a juicer. Pour juice into a tall glass over ice and serve.
**Makes 2 servings.**

## PEAR APPLE GRAPE JUICE

This fresh triple-fruit juice combination will guarantee a spectacular juice experience.

4-6 pears, peeled and cored
2-3 apples, peeled and cored
50g/2oz grapes

Run all the ingredients through a juicer. Pour juice into a tall glass over ice and serve.
**Makes 2 servings.**

# GERRY'S CHERRY JUICE

Oh my Gerry, he's as sweet as a cherry. **S**

115g/4oz cherries, pitted
1/4 fresh lime
115-225g/4-8oz green grapes

Run all the ingredients through a juicer. Pour juice into a tall glass over ice and serve.
**Makes 2 servings.**

# HOMEMADE VEGETABLE-8

Are you thinking you should have had something else? Maybe a healthy
Vegetable-8 juice?

This recipe is an impressive fusion of both fresh vegetables and seasonings.

4 medium carrots, peeled and cut into chunks
2 stalks celery, cut into chunks
3 small tomatoes, cut into chunks
50g/2oz fresh spinach
15g/1/2oz fresh parsley
1-2 spring onions

1/2 small beetroot, cut into chunks
1 clove garlic
1 tablespoon Braggs
pinch of dried oregano
tomato purée (optional)
Tabasco sauce (optional)

Run all the vegetables through a juicer. Stir in the Braggs and oregano, and a touch of tomato
purée if not thick enough, and pour juice into a tall glass over ice and serve. Spike it with a little
Tabasco for an added zip. **Makes 2 servings.**

# VEGAN BREAKFASTS

Breakfast! The most important meal of the day. As the recipes in this chapter demonstrate, there are a number of yummy vegan ways to start your morning.

# VEGETABLE TOFU SCRAMBLER

Did you know that adding tofu to your diet will protect you against heart disease and some cancers? Tofu is high in protein and calcium, low in fat and sodium, and cholesterol-free. See pg. 23 for more information on tofu. This recipe is great with toast, baked beans (pg. 93), and hashbrowns (pg. 41). **T**

1/2 medium onion, chopped
4-5 mushrooms, sliced
splash of olive oil
225g/8oz firm tofu, crumbled

1-2 teaspoons curry powder
pepper (to taste)
salsa (to taste)
2 spring onions, chopped

In a large saucepan, add the onions and mushrooms to a splash of oil and sauté on medium-high heat until the onions are translucent. Crumble tofu and add to saucepan. Add the curry and pepper. Sauté 10-12 minutes until moisture has evaporated. Add salsa and spring onions and scramble on high heat for 2-4 minutes.

**Note:** you could also add any other veggies you have kicking around. **Makes 2 or more servings.**

# GREEK SCRAMBLED TOFU

A delicious Mediterranean variation on scrambled tofu. Serve with toast and hashbrowns.

225g/8oz firm tofu, crumbled
1-2 tablespoons Braggs or soy sauce
turmeric (to taste)
pepper (to taste)
dried oregano (to taste)

splash of olive oil
6-8 Greek olives, chopped
handful of sun-dried tomatoes, chopped
25g/1oz spinach, chopped

In a large saucepan, add the tofu, Braggs, turmeric, pepper, and oregano to a splash of oil and sauté on medium-high heat for 10-12 minutes until moisture has evaporated. Add the olives, sun-dried tomatoes, and spinach. Cover and cook for 2-4 minutes, until spinach is tender. **Makes 2 or more servings.**

# SCRAMBLED EGGLESS EGGS

Light and satisfying.

1/2 medium onion, chopped
3 cloves garlic, crushed
splash of olive oil
225g/8oz medium tofu, crumbled

1/2 teaspoon turmeric
1/8 teaspoon cumin
2 tablespoons Braggs
gomashio (garnish) (pg. 154)

In a large saucepan, add the onions and garlic to a splash of oil and sauté on medium-high heat until onions are translucent. Add tofu, turmeric, cumin, and Braggs and mix together. Sauté on high heat for 5-10 minutes until tofu is lightly seared on one side. Stir and simmer on medium heat for 5-10 minutes until moisture has evaporated. Garnish with gomashio. **Makes 2 or more servings.**

# BARNARD'S BROWN RICE BREAKFAST

This is a great recipe if you have leftover rice. I love making this one for breakfast. It's fast, easy and oh so delicious. **T**

175g/6oz cooked brown rice
50g/2oz firm tofu
splash of olive oil

4 tablespoons soy mayonnaise (pg. 151)
4 slices bread
flax oil, Braggs, and ketchup (pg. 152) (garnish)

In a medium saucepan, add the rice and tofu to a splash of oil and sauté on medium-high heat until reasonably crisp. Toast bread and spread 1 tablespoon of the mayonnaise on each slice. Spoon the rice and tofu on top of toast and then garnish the way you like it. Eat and be happy. **Makes 2 or more servings.**

# HEARTY 3-GRAIN PORRIDGE

A hot, hardy grain cereal perfect for cold winter mornings. Serve with soy milk, maple syrup, and sliced bananas.

750ml/1 1/4 pints water
50g/2oz rolled oat flakes

50g/2oz barley
50g/2oz rice

In a medium pan, bring water to a boil. Add all the other ingredients. Lower heat and simmer for 45 minutes to an hour, stirring occasionally. **Makes 2 servings.**

# RACY RAISIN RICE PUDDING

This is a great recipe if you have leftover rice. Serve hot or cold with soy milk or cream.

475-750ml/16-22fl oz soy milk
350g/12oz cooked rice
1¹/₂ teaspoons cinnamon
1 tablespoon vanilla extract

150g/5oz raisins
50g/2oz slivered almonds
50g/2oz sweetener

In a medium saucepan, add the milk, cooked rice, cinnamon, vanilla, raisins, almonds, and sweetener and bring to a boil. Reduce heat and simmer on low heat for 15-20 minutes until pudding thickens to desired consistency, stirring occasionally. **Makes 2 or more servings.**

# CURRIED PAN-FRIED POTATOES

Don't have any orange juice to accompany your scrambled tofu? No problem: potatoes, eaten with the skins on, are a great source of vitamin C. Pan-fried potatoes are a great side dish for any breakfast entrée. So eat your spuds! Serve with baked beans (pg. 93) and toast.

1 medium onion, chopped
5 cloves garlic, chopped
1-2 teaspoons mustard seeds
1-2 teaspoons curry paste

splash of olive oil
3-6 medium potatoes, chopped
salt and pepper (to taste)

In a large saucepan, add the onions, garlic, mustard seeds, and curry paste to a splash of olive oil and sauté on medium heat until mixed well and onions are translucent. Add the potatoes and fry, flipping occasionally, until potatoes are soft enough to pierce with a fork. Season with salt and pepper to taste. **Makes 2 or more servings.**

# HEAVENLY HASHBROWNS

A new take on an old favourite. Pair with Vegetable Tofu Scrambler (pg. 39 ) and toast.

1 small onion, chopped
splash of olive oil
2 large potatoes, diced
6-8 mushrooms, diced

1 medium green pepper, diced
1 tablespoon dried dill
pepper and cracked chillies (to taste)

In a large saucepan, add the onions to splash of oil and sauté on medium high heat until translucent. Add the potatoes, mushrooms, green peppers, dill, pepper, and chillies. Turn down heat and cover until potatoes are soft enough to pierce with a fork. **Makes 2 or more servings.**

# CLASSIC PANCAKES

The best way to make pancakes is with a hot non-stick pan, a plastic spatula, and a lid to cover them while they cook, which hastens the cooking process and ensures that the middle won't end up gooey! Heat your oven to about 110°C/225°F/gas mark 1/4 and place a heat-resistant plate inside. As you finish making your pancakes, transfer them to the oven so that they'll stay warm until you are ready to serve them.

225g/8oz plain flour
1 teaspoon bicarbonate of soda
1 teaspoon baking powder

475ml/16fl oz soy milk
2 tablespoons oil
sliced fruit (garnish)

In a large bowl, sift the flour, bicarbonate of soda, and baking powder together. Add the milk and oil and mix together carefully until "just mixed" (if you mix too vigorously, the pancakes won't get fluffy!) Pour about 175-250ml/6-8fl oz of batter onto a hot non-stick pan or a lightly oiled frying pan and cover with a lid. Let sit on medium heat until the centre starts to bubble and becomes sturdy. Flip pancake over and cook other side until golden brown. Repeat process until all the batter is gone. Garnish with fresh fruit and maple syrup. **Makes 2 or more servings.**

# BRAINLESS BANANA PANCAKES

So yummy and sweet...you don't even need syrup!

115g/4oz plain flour
2 teaspoons baking powder
1 banana, mashed

300ml/1/2 pint soy milk
1 tablespoon sweetener
sliced fresh fruit (garnish)

In a large bowl, sift the flour and baking powder together. In a small bowl, mash the banana with a fork and add 50ml of the milk, mixing together until there are no lumps. Add the banana, sweetener, and remaining milk to the dry mix and stir together until "just mixed". Pour about 175-250ml/6-8fl oz of batter onto a hot non-stick pan or a lightly oiled frying pan and cover with a lid. Let sit on medium heat until the centre starts to bubble and become sturdy. Flip pancake over and cook other side until golden brown. Repeat process until all the batter is gone. Garnish with fresh fruit and maple syrup. **Makes 2 or more servings.**

# BASIC BUCKWHEAT PANCAKES

115g/4oz buckwheat flour
115g/4oz plain flour
1 tablespoon baking powder
1 teaspoon cinnamon

1 teaspoon vanilla extract
egg replacer (to equal 2 eggs)
115g/4oz apple sauce
475-600ml/16-20fl oz water

In a large bowl, stir together the flours, baking powder, and cinnamon until evenly blended. Add the vanilla, egg replacer, apple sauce, and water. Stir until "just mixed". Pour about 175-250ml/ 6-8fl oz of batter onto a hot non-stick pan or a lightly oiled frying pan and cover with a lid. Let sit on medium heat until the centre starts to bubble and become sturdy. Flip pancake over and cook other side until golden brown. Repeat process until all the batter is gone. **Makes 2 or more servings.**

# MONDAY MORNING OATMEAL PANCAKES

To make the oatmeal flour, blend 115g/4oz of rolled oat flakes in a blender or food processor.

115g/4oz oatmeal flour
115g/4oz rolled oat flakes
50g/2oz plain flour
1 teaspoon bicarbonate of soda

1 teaspoon salt
350ml/12fl oz sour soy milk (add 1 teaspoon vinegar
  to soy milk)
egg replacer (to equal 2 eggs)

In a large bowl, stir together the oatmeal flour, oat flakes, flour, bicarbonate of soda, and salt until evenly blended. Add the sour milk and egg replacer and stir until "just mixed". Pour about 175-250ml/6-8fl oz of batter onto a hot non-stick pan or a lightly oiled frying pan and cover with a lid. Let sit on medium heat until the centre starts to bubble and become sturdy. Flip pancake over and cook other side until golden brown. Repeat process until all the batter is gone. Top with maple syrup. **Makes 2 or more servings.**

# APPLE-CINNAMON CORNMEAL PANCAKES

40g/1½oz rolled oat flakes
75g/3oz cornmeal
75g/3oz plainflour
2 teaspoons baking powder

1 teaspoon cinnamon
4 tablespoons apple sauce
egg replacer (to equal 2 eggs)
475ml/16fl oz soy milk

In a large bowl, stir together the oat flakes, cornmeal, flour, baking powder, and cinnamon until evenly blended. Add the apple sauce, egg replacer, milk, and stir until "just mixed". Pour about 175-250ml/6-8fl oz of batter onto a hot non-stick pan or a lightly oiled frying pan and cover with a lid. Let sit on medium heat until the centre starts to bubble and become sturdy. Flip pancake over and cook other side until golden brown. Repeat process until all the batter is gone. Top with maple syrup. **Makes 2 or more servings.**

# FABULOUS FRENCH TOAST I

What's so French about this toast, anyway? This and the following recipe are both delicious and very easy to prepare. For extra flavour, try using raisin bread (pg. 119).

350ml/12fl oz soy milk
2 tablespoons plain flour
1 tablespoon nutritional yeast
1 teaspoon sweetener

1 teaspoon cinnamon
8-10 slices bread
fruit (garnish)

In a large bowl, whisk together the milk, flour, yeast, sweetener, and cinnamon vigorously. Soak 1 slice of bread in batter until bread is gooey. Fry in a non-stick pan or a lightly oiled frying pan on medium heat until golden. Flip and fry other side. Repeat until batter is gone. Garnish with fruit and maple syrup. **Makes 8-10 slices.**

# FABULOUS FRENCH TOAST II

This French toast is yeast-free for those with yeast allergies.

350ml/12fl oz soy milk
2 tablespoons plain flour
1 tablespoon psyllium husks
1 teaspoon sweetener

1 teaspoon cinnamon
5-10 bread slices
fruit (garnish)

In a large bowl, whisk together the milk, flour, psyllium husks, sweetener, and cinnamon vigorously. Let mixture sit for a spell so the psyllium has a chance to get eggy. Soak 1 slice of bread in batter until bread is gooey. Fry in a non-stick pan or a lightly oiled frying pan on medium heat until golden. Flip and fry other side. Repeat until batter is gone. Garnish with fruit and maple syrup. **Makes 5-10 slices.**

# RISE 'N SHINE MUESLI

Enjoy this healthy, crunchy muesli for breakfast, or any meal of the day. Once you try this recipe, you'll never want shop-bought again.

90-185g/3$^1$/$_2$-6$^1$/$_2$ oz rolled oat flakes
75g/3oz raw sunflower seeds
50g/2oz chopped almonds
50g/2oz sesame seeds
40g/1$^1$/$_2$ oz flax seeds
125ml/4fl oz oil
1 tablespoon carob powder or cocoa (optional)
1 teaspoon cinnamon

50-115g/2-4oz dry sweetener (you decide how sweet)
$^1$/$_2$ teaspoon salt
40g/1$^1$/$_2$ oz desiccated coconut
65g/2$^1$/$_2$ oz raisins
75g/3oz chopped dates
115g/4oz dried cranberries

Preheat oven to 180°C/350°F/gas mark 4. In a large bowl, mix together the oat flakes, sunflower seeds, almonds, sesame seeds, and flax seeds. In a medium-sized bowl, whisk together the oil, carob powder, cinnamon, sweetener, and salt. Add this mixture to the large bowl and combine well. In a roasting tin or on 2 baking sheets, spread mixture evenly and bake for 15-20 minutes, until the top layer is browned (if you use baking sheets, bake for 12-15 minutes). Flip over with a spatula and bake for another 8-10 minutes, then remove from oven. The mixture will be moist, but will dry and harden as it cools. Mix in dried fruit ingredients and let cool, stirring every 10 minutes to prevent clumping. Store in air-tight containers. Serve with fresh fruit and soy milk.

*You can throw anything you like into this: e.g., dried apricots, prunes, hemp seeds.

# "ANYTHING GOES" FRUIT-FILLED MUFFINS

Heaven knows... anything goes!

225g/8oz plain flour
1/2 teaspoon salt
3 teaspoons baking powder
115g/4oz sweetener
egg replacer (to equal 2 eggs)

4 tablespoons oil
175ml/6fl oz sour soy milk (add 1 teaspoon vinegar
   to soy milk)
175g/6oz fresh or frozen fruit of your choice

Preheat oven to 180°C/350°F/gas mark 4. In a large bowl, stir together the flour, salt, and baking powder. Add the sweetener, egg replacer, oil, sour milk, and fruit. Stir together until "just mixed." Scoop into lightly oiled muffin tins and bake for 35-45 minutes (use a fork to see if done).
**Makes 6 muffins.**

Here are some suggestions for fruit combinations for your muffins:

* apple, raisin
* banana, chocolate chip
* raspberry, blackberry
* strawberry, apricot
* pear, apple
* ginger, apple, apricot

See pgs. 123-125 for more muffin ideas.

# LIGHT APPLE BRAN MUFFINS

A nutritious way to start your day.

150g/5oz plain flour
75g/3oz bran
2 teaspoons baking powder
50g/2oz sweetener
1 tablespoon oil

150ml/1/4 pint soy milk
350ml/12fl oz apple sauce
1 teaspoon vanilla extract
1 banana

Preheat oven to 180°C/350°F/gas mark 4. In a large bowl, stir together the flour, bran, and baking powder. In a blender or food processor, blend the sweetener, oil, milk, apple sauce, vanilla, and banana. Add this to the flour mixture and stir together until "just mixed". Scoop into lightly oiled muffin tins and bake for 20-30 minutes (use a fork to see if done). **Makes 6 muffins.**

# MAKE YA GO BRAN MUFFINS

This is the perfect way to get the necessary fibre the body needs.

350g/12oz bran
350g/12oz plainflour
1 teaspoon bicarbonate of soda
1 teaspoon baking powder
115g/4oz sweetener

2 tablespoons molasses
125ml/4fl oz oil
350-475ml/12-16fl oz water
1 teaspoon vinegar
75g/3oz raisins or dates

Preheat oven to 180°C/350°F/gas mark 4. In a large bowl, stir together the bran, flour, bicarbonate of soda, and baking powder. Add the sweetener, molasses, oil, water, vinegar, and raisins. Stir together until "just mixed". Spoon into lightly oiled muffin tins and bake for 35-45 minutes (use a fork to see if done). **Makes 6-8 muffins.**

# FAUX EGGS BENNY

A vegan take on an old favourite. This is sure to be a hit.

450g/1lb medium tofu
4 tablespoons cider vinegar
4 tablespoons olive oil
1/4 teaspoon salt
4 English muffins or 8 slices of bread
8 slices of veggie back bacon
8 slices of tomato

**Sauce:**
40g/1 1/2 oz nutritional yeast
2 tablespoons flour
1/2 teaspoon salt
250ml/8fl oz water
1 tablespoon oil
1 teaspoon Braggs or soy sauce
2 teaspoons Dijon mustard

Preheat the oven to 230°C/450°F/gas mark 8. Drain tofu and cut into 8 slices. In a small bowl, whisk together the vinegar, oil, and salt. Arrange the tofu in a 15x23cm/6x9in baking dish and pour the oil and vinegar mixture over the top. Marinate for 15-30 minutes. Make sure to turn the tofu over occasionally so each side gets marinated. Then bake for 20 minutes or until crispy brown.

While tofu is baking, prepare the sauce. In a small saucepan, whisk the yeast, flour, and salt together. Add the water, oil, and Braggs and stir over medium heat until sauce starts to thicken. Stir in mustard and simmer on low heat until you are ready to serve. Toast the muffins or bread. On each slice of bread, place 1 piece of veggie bacon, 1 tofu piece, and 1 tomato slice, then cover with Benny sauce. **Makes 4 servings.**

# VEGAN SOUPS
# & STEWS

Soup is a universal meal, enhanced by regional and seasonal flavourings and diverse cooking methods. Here we offer some delicious soup variations. It is suggested that soups be made according to the season or the time of year; for example, hearty bean and grain soups and stews should be reserved for autumn and winter, while lighter, vegetable broth-like soups are best made during spring and summer. Enjoy all of our scrumptious soups and feel nourished.

# RUSTIC TOMATO LENTIL SOUP

This soup is quick and easy to prepare as lentils tend to cook more quickly than other beans. You can alter the look of this soup depending on your preference, since lentils come in a variety of colours – green, yellow, brown, or red. Cooked lentils are high in calcium, potassium, zinc, and iron.

as much garlic as you can stand, crushed
1 medium onion, diced
3 medium carrots, diced
2 tablespoons olive oil
2 stalks celery, chopped
1.5 litres/2½ pints vegetable stock (pg. 153)
2 x 400g cans chopped tomatoes, including juice or
    5-8 diced fresh tomatoes plus 4 tablespoons
    water

450g/1lb cooked or canned lentils
pepper (to taste)
cayenne pepper (to taste)
115g/4oz dry pasta (any short kind)

In a large saucepan, sauté garlic, onions, and carrots in oil on medium-high heat until the onions are translucent. Add the celery, stock, tomatoes, lentils, pepper, and cayenne pepper and bring to a boil. Reduce heat to low and simmer for 20 minutes or until carrots are tender. Add pasta and simmer for 10 more minutes before serving. **Makes 4-6 servings.**

# MIGHTY MISO SOUP

Miso is a fermented bean/grain paste that originated in Asia. There are 3 varieties of miso: soybean, barley, and brown rice; I like to use brown rice miso in this recipe because I find it has the best taste. Combining miso with shiitake mushrooms creates a balanced protein, which of course is a major concern among vegetarians and vegans alike. Shiitakes not only enhance the soup's flavour but also contain all 8 essential amino acids the body needs. A word of caution: NEVER boil or overcook your miso; this kills all of its nutrients. Always add your miso just before removing the soup from the heat. **T**

850ml/28fl oz water
115g/4oz medium or firm tofu, cubed
2 large shiitake mushrooms, chopped (or other mushrooms if not available)
3 tablespoons dried seaweed, chopped (hijiki is best)

2-3 heaped tablespoons miso paste (more or less to taste)
3 spring onions, chopped
3 tablespoons spinach, chopped (or kale, pak choi, or Swiss chard)

In a medium saucepan, add the water, tofu, mushrooms and dried seaweed and bring to a boil on medium-high heat. Reduce heat and simmer for 5-8 minutes, until mushrooms are tender. Remove from heat, stir in the miso, onions, and spinach and let sit for another 30 seconds. **Makes 4 servings.**

# SWEET POTATO, SQUASH, & APPLE SOUP

This soup is perfect for those autumn days when the sun sets a little earlier than the day before. The squash and apple complement one another quite nicely in this soup. Sweet potatoes and yams are loaded with vitamins A and C and potassium.

1 medium onion, chopped
1 tablespoon olive oil
475ml/16fl oz vegetable stock (pg. 153)
350g/12oz butternut squash, peeled and diced
350g/12oz sweet potatoes or yams, peeled and diced
2-3 medium apples, cored and diced

1/2 teaspoon salt
1/2 teaspoon pepper
1/2 teaspoon nutmeg
1/4 teaspoon cayenne pepper

In a large saucepan, sauté the onions in oil on medium-high heat until translucent. Add the stock, squash, potatoes, apples, and salt, pepper, nutmeg, and cayenne pepper and bring to a boil. Turn down heat and simmer for 30 minutes. Take 2 ladles' worth of vegetables and 1 ladle of stock and blend in blender or food processor until smooth. Return to the pan and stir together before serving. **Makes 4-6 servings.**

# GINGER PEANUT SOUP

Did you know that peanuts are not really nuts but are actually a type of bean? Peanuts are sprayed with an array of pesticides and herbicides, so try and use organic peanut butter in this recipe. It will taste better.

175g/6oz broccoli, chopped
175g/6oz cauliflower, chopped
1 medium onion, chopped
1 tablespoon fresh ginger, grated
3 cloves garlic, chopped
1/4 teaspoon cayenne pepper

1/2 teaspoon salt
1/2 teaspoon pepper
2 tablespoons olive oil
750ml/1¼ pints vegetable stock or water
2 x 400g cans chopped tomatoes
5 tablespoons natural peanut butter (or nut butter)

In a large pan, sauté the broccoli, cauliflower, onions, ginger, garlic, cayenne pepper, salt, and pepper in oil on medium heat until vegetables are tender. Add the stock, tomatoes, and nut butter. Reduce heat and simmer for 20 minutes, stirring occasionally. **Makes 4-6 servings.**

# MULLIGATAWNY SOUP

A creamy Indian soup flavoured with just the right amount of spices.

1 large onion, chopped
3 stalks celery, chopped
3 tablespoons olive oil
1/2 teaspoon cayenne pepper
1 teaspoon turmeric
1 teaspoon coriander
1 teaspoon curry powder
2 tablespoons Braggs or soy sauce
1.5 litres/2½ pints vegetable stock or water
2 medium carrots, sliced

2 large potatoes, cut in cubes
90g/3½ oz rice
1 small red pepper, diced
1 small green pepper, diced
1 small tomato, diced
115g/4oz cauliflower, sliced
65g/2½ oz desiccated coconut
3 teaspoons lemon juice
3 teaspoons coriander (optional)

In a large saucepan, sauté the onions and celery in oil on medium heat until onions are translucent. Add the cayenne pepper, turmeric, coriander, curry, Braggs, stock, carrots, potatoes, and rice. Bring to a boil and reduce heat. Let simmer for 15-20 minutes. Add the peppers, tomato, cauliflower, coconut, lemon juice, and coriander. Stir together and simmer 5-10 more minutes until vegetables are tender. Remove half of soup and blend in blender or food processor. Return to the pan and mix together. **Makes 4-6 servings.**

# SPICY CREAMY TOMATO SOUP

Is the tomato a fruit or a vegetable? Most people would say a vegetable, but it's actually a fruit, given that it's a flowering plant containing seeds. Tomatoes are an excellent source of vitamin C and A. This soup is just like Grandma used to make.

1 medium onion, finely chopped
6 cloves garlic, crushed
1/2 teaspoon salt
1 teaspoon dried dill
1 teaspoon pepper or cayenne pepper
1 tablespoon olive oil

400g can chopped tomatoes or 2-4 fresh tomatoes, diced plus 4 tablespoons water
475ml/16fl oz vegetable stock or water
1 tablespoon sweetener
115g/4oz soft or silken tofu or 125ml/4fl oz soy milk
2 medium fresh tomatoes, diced (garnish)

In a large saucepan, sauté the onions, garlic, salt, dill, and pepper in oil on medium heat until onions are translucent. Add the tomatoes, stock, and sweetener. Cover and simmer over low heat for 20 minutes. In a blender or food processor, blend tofu and 350ml/12fl oz of broth until smooth. Add to soup pot and stir in freshly diced tomatoes. **Makes 4-6 servings.**

# HEARTY WINTER POTATO SOUP

Potatoes are highly nutritious, an excellent source of vitamins B and C as well as minerals like magnesium and iron. Potatoes are also known to be one of the best sources of complex carbohydrates, noted for having a calming effect on the body and mind. **Tip on storing potatoes: cover them with a dark sheet or cloth and store them in a cool, dark, dry place. This prevents light from penetrating the potatoes and causing them to turn green and sprout.**

1 medium onion, chopped
3 cloves garlic, chopped
4-6 mushrooms, chopped
2 tablespoons olive oil
4-5 medium potatoes, cubed
750ml/1¼ pints vegetable stock or water
1 red pepper, sliced
pinch of red chilli flakes

1/2 teaspoon coriander
1 teaspoon cumin
1 teaspoon dried basil
1/4 teaspoon pepper
2 teaspoons Braggs or soy sauce
250ml/8fl oz soy milk
2 spring onions, sliced (garnish)
croutons (garnish) (pg. 152)

In a large saucepan, sauté the onions, garlic, and mushrooms in oil on medium heat until onions become translucent. Add the potatoes, stock, red pepper, red chilli flakes, coriander, cumin, basil, pepper, and Braggs. Bring to a boil and reduce heat. Simmer on low heat for 10-20 minutes until potatoes are tender. Remove 2 ladles' worth of vegetables and blend in blender or food processor with milk until smooth. Add the mixture back to the soup and simmer for 5 more minutes. Do not boil or it will burn! Garnish with spring onions and serve with croutons. **Makes 4-6 servings.**

# AUNTIE BONNIE'S CURRIED APPLE SOUP

My Auntie Bonnie can make a wicked soup out of almost any ingredient. **S**

1 large onion, chopped
1 apple, peeled and chopped
2 tablespoons olive oil
2 teaspoons curry powder
750ml-1litre/1¼-1¾ pints vegetable stock
   or water

275g/10oz mixed vegetables of your choice, diced
   (e.g., courgette, asparagus, broccoli)
50g/2oz rice
salt (to taste)
pepper (to taste)

In a medium pan, sauté the onions and apple in oil on medium heat until onions become translucent. Sprinkle with curry powder; stir well. Pour in the vegetable stock and bring to a boil. Add the vegetables, rice, salt, and pepper; cover and simmer on low heat for about 30 minutes, until rice and vegetables are tender. In a blender or food processor, blend half or all of soup until smooth; return to pot and reheat. **Makes 4-6 servings.**

# SIMPLY LOVELY CARROT SOUP

Use well-washed, unpeeled organic carrots in this recipe. The peel is where most of the nutrients reside, such as carotene (which the body converts into vitamin A), fibre, and calcium. It also makes this soup taste sweeter and more flavourful.

1 small onion, chopped
6-8 large carrots, chopped
2 tablespoons olive oil
1 litre/1¾ pints vegetable stock or water
1 teaspoon salt

250ml/8fl oz soy milk
1 teaspoon dried dill (or 1 tablespoon fresh dill)
1 tablespoon Braggs or soy sauce
½ teaspoon pepper

In a large saucepan, sauté the onions and carrots in oil on medium heat until the onions become translucent. Add the stock and salt and simmer over medium heat for about 15 minutes, until carrots are tender. Remove half of the vegetables and blend in a blender or food processor with the milk, dill, Braggs, and pepper, and a small amount of cooking broth until smooth. Return mixture to the pan, mix well, and serve immediately. **Makes 4-6 servings.**

# TORTILLA CHIP SOUP

This soup is deceptively simple. But it's amazing with crumbled tortilla chips and avocado slices!

1 small onion, chopped
3 cloves garlic, chopped
2 tablespoons olive oil
750ml/1¼ pints vegetable stock or water
2 x 400g cans chopped tomatoes or 5-8 fresh tomatoes, diced plus 4 tablespoons water

2 tablespoons tomato purée
2 jalapeño chillies, seeded and finely chopped
2 teaspoons cumin
2 teaspoons chilli powder
tortilla chips, crushed (garnish)
avocado slices (garnish)

In a large saucepan, sauté the onions and garlic in oil on medium heat until onions are translucent. Add the stock, tomatoes, paste, jalapeños, cumin, and chilli powder. Simmer for 20-30 minutes. Garnish with crushed chips and avocado slices. **Makes 4-6 servings.**

# BUTTERNUT TOMATO SOUP

Autumn captured in a soup. Butternut squash, a variety of winter squash, is spectacular in soups.

4-6 cloves garlic, crushed
1 tablespoon fresh ginger, grated
1 medium butternut squash, peeled and cubed
1 tablespoon olive oil
250ml/8fl oz vegetable stock or water
2 x 400g cans chopped tomatoes or 5-8 fresh tomatoes, diced plus 4 tablespoons water

salt (to taste)
pepper (to taste)
250ml/8fl oz soy milk
croutons (garnish) (pg. 152)
2-3 spring onions, chopped (garnish)

In a large pan, sauté the garlic, ginger, and squash in oil on low-medium heat until the garlic is softened. Add the stock, tomatoes, and salt, and pepper. Simmer on medium heat, stirring frequently, for 15-20 minutes or until squash can be pierced easily with a fork. Blend half of the vegetables with the milk in a blender or food processor. Return to soup and simmer 5 minutes more. Garnish with croutons and spring onions. **Makes 4-6 servings.**

# MOMMA SARAH'S MATZO BALL SOUP

Matzo balls can be made before-hand and refrigerated for use later. Just remember not to warm up the matzo balls in your broth; use a separate pot of warm water, and then add them to the soup bowl just before serving. You can use matzo balls in all sorts of different soups. This simple broth is my favourite. It reminds me of the soup my dad used to make me whenever I had a cold. This recipe has been adapted for all of us vegan Jews. **S**

## Simple Broth:
2 medium carrots, chopped
splash of olive oil
1 litre/1³/4 pints vegetable stock
3 spring onions, chopped*
50g/2oz peas

In a medium pan, sauté the carrots in a splash of oil for 5-8 minutes on medium heat until tender. Add the stock, onions, and peas and simmer for another 5 minutes. Pour into bowls and then add your matzo balls. **Makes 2 servings.**

*You can add any other vegetables you like to this broth. When I make this when I'm ill, I like to keep it simple.

## Matzo Balls:
50g/2oz matzo meal
2 tablespoons potato flour
1 teaspoon salt
150ml/1/4 pint vegetable stock or water

In a medium bowl, stir together the matzo meal, starch and salt. Add the stock and stir together well. Cover bowl and place in refrigerator for 20-30 minutes. Once chilled, roll about 1 tablespoon of dough into a ball. Set aside and repeat until all the dough is gone. Bring a medium pan of salted water to a brisk boil. Reduce heat to medium-low, drop balls into water, and boil gently for 20 minutes, making sure they don't stick together. Keep an eye on them, because if the water boils too vigorously the balls will fall apart. A good indication that they are done is when they float to the top of the pan. **Makes 10-12 balls.** Have broth ready in bowls. Remove matzo balls with a slotted spoon and place in broth.

# GARDEN VEGETABLE BORSCHT

This bright, eye-catching soup is bursting with fresh vegetable goodness.

1 small red onion, chopped
4 cloves garlic, crushed
2 large carrots, chopped
2-4 medium beetroot, chopped
2 tablespoons olive oil
115g/4oz cabbage, chopped

50g/2oz spinach, chopped
2 x 400g cans chopped tomatoes or 5-8 fresh
   tomatoes, diced plus 4 tablespoons water
600ml/1 pint vegetable stock or water
1/4 teaspoon pepper
1/4 teaspoon horseradish sauce (optional)

In a large saucepan, sauté the onion, garlic, carrots, and beetroot in oil on medium heat until onions are translucent. Add the cabbage, spinach, tomatoes, stock, pepper, and horseradish. Simmer on medium heat for 20-30 minutes or until carrots and beetroot can be pierced easily with a fork. Serve with warm fresh biscuits (pg. 116) and tofu sour cream (pg. 152). **Makes 4-6 servings.**

# CHIVE BUTTERNUT SOUP

A colourful and zesty soup. Chives add a subtle flavour that is sure to please.

1 small onion, chopped
1-2 stalks celery, chopped
250g/9oz butternut squash, peeled and cubed
2 tablespoons olive oil
475ml/16fl oz stock or water

150g/5oz cooked or canned cannellini beans
1 teaspoon pepper
1/2 teaspoon salt
15g/1/2 oz chives, snipped

In a medium saucepan, sauté the onions, celery, and squash in oil on medium-high heat until onions are translucent. Add the stock, beans, pepper, and salt. Simmer on medium-low heat for 15 minutes, then remove from heat. Remove half of the vegetables and broth and blend in a blender or food processor until smooth. Return to pan and stir in chives. **Makes 2 servings.**

# JANA'S SPRING GARDEN SOUP

Get outside, plant a garden, and enjoy the fruits of your labour.

2 litres/3 1/2 pints water

115g/4oz each of as many of the following
fresh greens:
- nettles
- spring greens, sliced into strips
- kale, roughly chopped
- mustard greens, roughly chopped
- Swiss chard, roughly chopped

25g/1oz dandelion greens, roughly chopped
2 medium carrots, chopped
3 spring onions, chopped
sprig of fresh fennel
450g/1lb medium tofu, cubed
1 teaspoon Braggs or soy sauce
4 tablespoons miso

In a large saucepan, bring the water to boil. Add the greens, dandelions, carrots, onions, and fennel and simmer for 20-30 minutes on medium heat. Stir in the tofu, Braggs, and miso and remove from heat. Let stand 10 minutes before serving. **Makes 4-6 servings.**

# JANA'S WINTER SICKY SOUP

When winter has you sniffling and sneezing, strain the broth from this soup and drink as much as you can all day long. If you're not sick but just want a wonderful soup to get you through the winter blues, Jana's hearty soup will do the trick.

1/2 medium butternut squash, peeled and cubed
4 medium carrots, sliced
50-115g/2-4oz burdock roots, sliced
1/2 dandelion root, chopped
2 tablespoons olive oil
1/2 medium white onion, chopped
4 tablespoons fresh ginger, grated
8 cloves fresh garlic, chopped
2 litres/3 1/2 pints vegetable stock or water

1 teaspoon cayenne pepper
1 teaspoon curry powder
pinch of salt
2 tablespoons fresh rosemary, chopped
3 lemon slices
4 whole leaves of spring greens, roughly chopped
4 tablespoons miso
1 spring onion, chopped (garnish)

In a large saucepan, sauté the squash, carrots, and burdock and dandelion roots in oil on medium-high heat for 5-10 minutes or until ingredients are tender. Add the onions, ginger, and garlic and cook 5 minutes more. Pour in the stock and add the cayenne pepper, curry, salt, rosemary, lemon, and spring greens and simmer on medium-low heat for 40 minutes. Remove from heat, stir in miso, and let stand 5 minutes before serving. Garnish with spring onions. **Makes 4-6 servings.**

# MUSHROOM BARLEY STEW

Barley is a rugged grain that has been used for food, barter, and beer for over 4,000 years. It is a nutritionally balanced food high in protein and carbohydrates. It also provides a great deal of bulk by absorbing 2-3 times its volume of the cooking liquid. Having a mild taste but a chewy texture, it is a pleasant addition to this stew.

1 medium carrot, chopped
1/2 medium onion, sliced
2 large cloves garlic, crushed
1/2 medium green pepper, chopped
1/2 medium red pepper, chopped
2 tablespoons olive oil
15-20 small mushrooms, chopped
200g/7oz dry pearl barley

65g/21/2 oz cooked or canned chickpeas
1 teaspoon cumin
splash of Tabasco sauce (to taste)
salt (to taste)
pepper (to taste)
1 tablespoon Braggs or soy sauce
750ml-1 litre/11/4-13/4 pints vegetable stock

In a large saucepan sauté the carrots, onions, garlic, and peppers in oil on medium heat until onions are translucent. Add the mushrooms and sauté until the mushrooms become tender. Add the barley, chickpeas, cumin, Tabasco, salt, pepper, Braggs, and stock and simmer for 20-30 minutes until barley is cooked. Serve with warm biscuits (pg. 116). **Makes 4-6 servings.**

# GARDEN MEDLEY VEGETABLE STEW

The most delicious stew ever. Too nutritious to mention all of its wholesome properties, you're just going to have to make this savoury stew and find out for yourself. You could also throw in whatever vegetables you have in your fridge – the more, the merrier!

1/2 medium onion, chopped
3 cloves garlic, crushed
2 medium carrots, chopped
1 tablespoon olive oil
1/2 butternut squash, peeled and cubed
1 medium potato, chopped
1/2 medium green pepper, cored and chopped

2 x 400g cans chopped tomatoes and juice or 5-8
   fresh tomatoes, diced plus 4 tablespoons water
1 teaspoon balsamic vinegar
475ml/16fl oz vegetable stock or water
1 teaspoon turmeric
1 teaspoon cumin
1 teaspoon chilli powder

In a large saucepan, sauté the onions, garlic, and carrots in oil on medium heat until onions are translucent. Add the squash, potato, pepper, tomatoes, vinegar, stock, and turmeric, cumin, and chilli powder. Simmer for 30-45 minutes until vegetables are tender, and serve.
**Makes 4-6 servings.**

# AUNTIE BONNIE'S LIVELY LENTIL STEW

1 large onion, chopped
2 stalks celery, diced
2 medium carrots, chopped
1 tablespoon olive oil
225g/8oz dry green lentils
750ml/1¼ pints vegetable stock or water
2 x 400g cans chopped tomatoes and juice or 5-8
   fresh tomatoes, diced plus 4 tablespoons water

2 tablespoons tomato purée
1 small potato, diced
½ teaspoon red chilli flakes
½ teaspoon salt
½ teaspoon pepper
25g/1oz spinach, chopped
3 tablespoons fresh parsley, chopped

In a large saucepan, sauté the onions, celery, and carrots in oil on medium heat until onions are translucent. Add the lentils, stock, tomatoes, tomato purée, potatoes, red chilli flakes, salt, and pepper. Bring to a boil and simmer gently for 30-45 minutes, stirring frequently until lentils are tender. Stir in spinach and parsley and simmer for 5 minutes more. **Makes 4-6 servings.**

# VEGAN SALADS
# & DRESSINGS

# SALADS

Long gone are the days when salads consisted only of iceberg lettuce and tomato slices, slathered with bottled dressing. It's time to welcome a beautiful array of fresh, wholesome salads with tantalizing tastes into your diet. Salads offer the freshest, most wholesome food nutrients available. Raw salad is especially beneficial because our bodies digest nutrients and enzymes more readily than if the ingredients were cooked. These salads can be served to accompany meals or as meals on their own.

# TANYA'S GARDEN MEDLEY

I love making this huge salad and feasting on it for days. I combine every vegetable in my refrigerator for this creation. Feel the goodness of all these vegetables racing through your veins, giving you the energy you need to live in this crazy world. **T**

1 head red leaf lettuce, roughly chopped
1 bunch spinach, roughly chopped
115g/4oz red cabbage, shredded
1 small beetroot, grated
5-10 mushrooms, sliced
4-5 spring onions, sliced

3-4 medium carrots, sliced
1 medium cucumber, sliced
handful sunflower sprouts
115g/4oz broccoli sprouts
115g/4oz mixed bean sprouts
3 tablespoons gomashio (pg.154)

Wash and prepare all vegetables. In a large bowl, toss together the lettuce and spinach. Add the other ingredients and toss. Store the uneaten portion in a covered bowl in the refrigerator. Keeps crisp for up to 3 or 4 days. Eat as is or add the dressing of your choice. **Makes 4-6 servings.**

# JANA'S GARDEN KITCHEN SALAD

Our friend Jana from Earth's Herbal Products is an amazing woman. Not only does she have a vast knowledge of herbs and plants and their medicinal qualities, she's also a whizz in the kitchen.

5 whole kale leaves, roughly chopped
1 handful rocket leaves (including the flowers),
   roughly chopped
3 whole leaves of mustard greens, roughly chopped
1/2 head butterhead lettuce, roughly chopped
4 tablespoons coriander, chopped
4 tablespoons spring onions, finely chopped
2 sprigs of fresh fennel, finely chopped

10 almonds
seasonal edible flowers (throw petals in whole)
   (optional):
   - 5 rose petals
   - 10 borage flowers (purple)
   - 3 honeysuckle flowers
   - 1 calendula flower

Wash and prepare all vegetables. In a large bowl toss together all the ingredients. Serve with Jana's Famous Herb Dressing (pg. 73). **Makes 4-6 servings.**

# GOURMET GREEK SALAD

Here's a salad of mythological proportions. This combination of vegetables, faux feta, and saucy seasoning would bring a smile even to the face of Zeus.

6-8 plum tomatoes, quartered
1 small cucumber, sliced
1 small red pepper, sliced
1 small green pepper, sliced

1 small yellow pepper, sliced
1 small red onion, sliced
Greek olives (optional)
450g/1lb faux feta (pg. 155)

Prepare the vegetables and place in a serving bowl. Add the faux feta and remaining feta marinade to the salad ingredients just before serving. Toss well. **Makes 4-6 servings.**

# VEGETABLE PASTA SALAD

Simple, cool, and delicious, this salad is refreshing and lively. Perfect picnic food.

600-800g/1lb 6oz-1³/4 lb cooked pasta (e.g., penne, macaroni, fusilli)
3 tablespoons flax oil
1 small courgette, sliced
4 tablespoons lemon juice
1 tablespoon olive oil
3 spring onions, chopped
1/2 medium green pepper, chopped

2 medium tomatoes, chopped
115g/4oz snow peas, chopped in half
15g/¹/2 oz fresh parsley, chopped
1 tablespoon fresh basil
1/2 teaspoon salt
pepper (to taste)
50g/2oz faux Parmesan cheese (pg. 154)

In a medium saucepan, cook pasta until al dente (tender but still firm to bite). Drain and rinse pasta under cold water until cool. Transfer to a large bowl. In a small bowl, whisk together the flax oil and lemon juice. Stir into the pasta and set aside.

In a large saucepan, sauté the courgette in oil on medium-low heat for 3 minutes. Add the onions, peppers, tomatoes, mangetout, parsley, basil, salt, and pepper. Sauté for 3-5 minutes.
Add the vegetable mixture and the Parmesan to the pasta and toss well. Chill before serving.
**Makes 4-6 servings.**

# FAUX CHICKEN SALAD

The following three "mock" salad recipes are just as impressive alone as they are when served between bread as sandwich fillings.

225g/8oz tempeh, cubed*
125ml/4fl oz soy mayonnaise (pg. 151)
1 stalk celery, finely chopped
1 medium gherkin, finely chopped
1/2 medium onion, chopped

2 tablespoons fresh parsley, finely chopped
2 teaspoons mustard
2 teaspoons Braggs or soy sauce
1 garlic clove, crushed and finely chopped

Steam the cubed tempeh for 15 minutes on medium-high heat. Remove from heat and set aside to cool. In a medium bowl, combine the mayonnaise, celery, gherkin, onion, parsley, mustard, Braggs, and garlic with the tempeh and toss lightly. Serve over toast, as a side dish, as a sandwich filling, or alone. (For a variation, add 1-2 teaspoons of curry powder to spice it up a bit!) **Makes 2-4 servings.**

*If you have trouble finding tempeh, you can use firm tofu, but it's not quite as effective.

# FAUX TUNA SALAD

You can find kelp powder in health food shops. Serve this on toast or as a side dish.

450g/1lb firm tofu, frozen and then thawed
1 stalk celery, diced
1/4 medium red onion, chopped
1 small carrot, finely chopped

125ml/4fl oz soy mayonnaise (pg. 151)
2 tablespoons Braggs or soy sauce
1/2 tablespoon lemon juice or vinegar
1/2-3/4 teaspoon kelp powder

Freezing tofu will give it a chewy, meaty texture. See pg. 23 for instructions. Once thawed, squeeze the excess moisture out and crumble it into small pieces. In a medium bowl, combine the tofu, celery, onion, and carrot. Stir in the mayonnaise, Braggs, lemon juice, and kelp and mix together well. **Makes 2-4 servings.**

# FAUX EGG SALAD

450g/1lb medium tofu, mashed
125ml/4fl oz soy mayonnaise (pg. 151)
4 tablespoons chopped parsley
1-2 gherkins, diced or 4 tablespoons relish
1 1/2 tablespoons mustard

1-2 spring onions, chopped
2 stalks celery, diced
2 cloves garlic, crushed
1 1/2 teaspoons salt
1/4 teaspoon turmeric

In a medium bowl, mash the tofu with your hands or fork and add the remaining ingredients. Mix together well and chill before serving. **Makes 2-4 servings.**

# EXQUISITE RICE SALAD

A lovely, tangy salad that goes great with any meal.

1 tablespoon olive oil
2 teaspoons mustard seeds
2 teaspoons cumin seeds
2-4 garlic cloves, crushed
1 teaspoon fresh ginger, grated
1 teaspoon turmeric
1/8 teaspoon cayenne pepper
600ml/1 pint water
1 cinnamon stick

200g/7oz long-grain brown rice
3 tablespoons rice vinegar
2 tablespoons dark sesame oil
2 tablespoons Braggs or soy sauce
4 tablespoons flax oil
1 medium carrot, finely chopped
75g/3oz raisins
4 spring onions, chopped
50g/2oz peas

In a large saucepan, heat the oil over medium heat. Add the mustard seeds, cumin, garlic, ginger, turmeric, and cayenne pepper. Stir until mustard seeds begin to pop (about 30 seconds), then add water and cinnamon. Cover and bring to a boil.

Add rice to the pan and cover. Reduce heat to low and simmer about 35-40 minutes, until rice is done. Remove the pan from heat and let stand for 10 minutes. Remove the cinnamon stick.

In a small bowl, whisk together the vinegar, sesame oil, Braggs, and flax oil until combined. Pour onto the rice, add the carrots, raisins, onions, and peas. Stir until well mixed. Transfer to bowl and chill before serving. **Makes 4-6 servings.**

# COUSIN NATASHA'S RICE & BEAN SALAD

This is my cousin's supper trademark. Our family loves to get together and share food; we eat and eat and eat. My favourite things are: food, family, friends, and fun. **S**

200g/7oz cooked rice
1 large red onion, diced
2 or more medium tomatoes, diced
1 medium red pepper, diced
1/2 medium green pepper, diced
175g/6oz sweetcorn
275g/10oz cooked or canned kidney beans

1 avocado, diced
6-10 sprigs coriander, chopped
2 tablespoons red wine vinegar
dash of cayenne pepper
juice of one lemon
dash of Tabasco (to taste)

Wash and prepare all the vegetables and place them and the other ingredients in a medium bowl. Stir together well and chill before serving. **Makes 4-6 servings.**

# MUM'S APPLE COLESLAW SALAD

This recipe was adapted from an old recipe of my mum's. When I eat it, I feel like I'm eight years old. **S**

1/2 small white cabbage, shredded
2-3 apples, grated or chopped
75g/3oz raisins

125ml/4fl oz soy mayonnaise (pg. 151)
1 teaspoon caraway
dash of lemon juice

Place the cabbage, apples, and raisins in a medium bowl. Add the mayonnaise, caraway, and lemon juice. Mix together well and chill before serving. **Makes 4-6 servings.**

# SESAME NOODLE SALAD

The flavour of sesame oil is the subtle surprise in this tasty creation. An elegant, satisfying salad.

buckwheat noodles (to serve 4)
2 tablespoons sesame oil
4 tablespoons Braggs
4 tablespoons rice vinegar
50g/2oz cucumber, seeded and shredded

50g/2oz carrots, peeled and shredded
6 large radishes, sliced
3 spring onions, thinly sliced
2-4 tablespoons gomashio (pg.154) (garnish)

In a medium pan, cook noodles until al dente (tender but still firm to bite), about 8 minutes. Drain and rinse noodles under cold water until cool. Transfer to a large bowl. In a small bowl, whisk together the sesame oil, Braggs, and vinegar. Toss with the noodles to coat. Add the cucumber, carrots, radishes, and onions, and toss. Garnish with gomashio.

# TENACIOUS TABOULI

Bulgur is a dried form of cooked, cracked wheat. Nutritious and delicious, it gives this exquisite salad a chewy texture.

850ml/28fl oz boiling water
350g/12oz uncooked bulgur or couscous
3 stalks celery, chopped
4-6 spring onions, chopped
2 medium carrots, chopped
3 large tomatoes, chopped
4 tablespoons flax oil

5 tablespoons lemon juice
40g/1 1/2 oz fresh parsley, chopped
1 tablespoon fresh mint, chopped
1 1/2 teaspoons salt
1/8 teaspoon cayenne pepper
2-4 cloves garlic, crushed
115g/4oz cooked or canned chickpeas

In a medium bowl, pour boiling water over the bulgur. Set aside and let sit for 30 minutes. Meanwhile, prepare vegetables and set aside. Drain off excess water from the bulgur and add the vegetables, oil, lemon juice, parsley, mint, salt, cayenne pepper, garlic, and chickpeas. Toss together well and chill before serving.

# AUNTIE BONNIE'S POTATO CUCUMBER SALAD

This tangy, tart salad will tickle your tastebuds.

350-475g/12oz-1lb 2oz new potatoes, cubed
1 tablespoon fresh dill, chives or parsley, chopped
1 tablespoon Dijon mustard
2 tablespoons red wine vinegar
1 tablespoon horseradish sauce

4 tablespoons flax oil
1/4 teaspoon salt
1/4 teaspoon pepper
225-350g/8-12oz cucumber, cubed

In a medium pan, boil the cubed potatoes in water until they can be pierced easily with a fork. In a small bowl, whisk together the chosen herb, mustard, vinegar, horseradish, oil, salt, and pepper. Set aside. Once the potatoes are done, drain and rinse under cold water until cool. In a medium bowl, mix together the potatoes, cucumbers, and dressing just before serving. **Makes 4-6 servings.**

# S & M SPICY SALAD

My cousin Stacy and his partner Molly passed this recipe on to me. This salad rocks! S

450g/1lb firm tofu, cubed
2 medium carrots, chopped
6-8 green beans, cut into 5cm/2in slices
600g/1lb 6oz butternut squash, peeled and cubed
5-8 mushrooms, chopped
1/2-1 teaspoon red chilli flakes or cayenne pepper
2 tablespoons olive oil

1 small red onion, chopped
1 small red pepper, chopped
1 small cucumber, chopped
handful spicy Japanese sprouts
1-2 teaspoons wasabi
25g/1oz faux Parmesan cheese (pg. 154)
3 tablespoons rice vinegar

In a medium-sized pan, sauté the tofu, carrots, green beans, squash, mushrooms, and red chilli flakes in oil on medium-high heat for about 8-12 minutes, until the squash can be pierced easily with a fork. Stir occasionally. Set aside.

In a medium bowl, place the onions, peppers, cucumbers, and sprouts. In a small bowl, whisk together the wasabi, Parmesan, and vinegar. Add the cooked ingredients to the fresh vegetables. Toss with the wasabi dressing right before serving. If you want to add some weight to this salad, serve over a bowl of rice. **Makes 4-6 servings.**

# PERFECT POTATO SALAD

Simple, cool, and delicious — perfect for picnics.

850g/1lb 14oz potatoes, cubed
1 teaspoon salt
1 teaspoon sweetener
1 teaspoon celery seeds
2 teaspoons vinegar
3-5 spring onions, chopped

3 stalks celery, chopped
2 gherkins, chopped
350ml/12fl oz soy mayonnaise (pg. 151)
1/2-1 teaspoon Dijon mustard
115g/4oz medium tofu, crumbled

In a large pan, boil the cubed potatoes in water until they can be pierced easily with a fork. Drain and rinse under cold water until cool. Once potatoes are room temperature, place them in a large bowl, and add the rest of the ingredients. Mix well and chill before serving. **Makes 4-6 servings.**

# AMAZING AMBROSIA SALAD

The food of the Gods: need we say more?

90g/3 1/2 oz pineapple, chopped
90g/3 1/2 oz apples, chopped
90g/3 1/2 oz oranges, chopped
115g/4oz strawberries, sliced
115g/4oz grapes
40g/1 1/2 oz desiccated coconut, shredded
1 tablespoon cornflour

6 tablespoons lemon juice
3 tablespoons dry sweetener
3 tablespoons orange juice
115g/4oz soft tofu, puréed
2 teaspoons orange rind, grated
1 teaspoon poppy seeds (optional)

In a large bowl, toss the fruit and coconut until well mixed and refrigerate. In a medium saucepan combine the cornflour with the lemon juice and stir until well blended. Place the saucepan over low heat and add the sweetener and orange juice. Cook for about 5 to 10 minutes, stirring constantly, until mixture thickens. Remove the saucepan from the heat and allow to cool thoroughly. In a blender or food processor, purée the tofu, then stir in the orange rind and poppy seeds. Add this to the juice mixture and chill for at least 1 hour. Pour the dressing over the fruit immediately before serving. **Makes 4-6 servings.**

# DRESSINGS

Delicious and nutritious dressings depend on the use of the finest ingredients possible. Try to use only cold pressed oil in these recipes, as they contain essential fatty acids needed by the body. Vary your oils by using olive, flax, hemp, canola, sunflower, or sesame; in this way it's possible to get a healthy balance of Omega-3 and Omega-6 in the diet. Some of these dressings have a distinct flavour, so experiment and see which ones you prefer.

# PRETTY 'N PINK CHIVE VINEGAR

My Auntie Bonnie gave me this great idea for a vinegar. When your chives are in full bloom, remove the purple flower tops and cram as many as you can into a clean, dry jar. Pour in white wine vinegar and fill to the top. Cap tightly and let sit in a cool dark spot for 3-5 days. Strain out the flower tops and store the remaining vinegar in a clean, sealable container. Use this lovely, scented, pink vinegar for your salads. **S**

# ROASTED GARLIC DRESSING

The perfect topping for enhancing any salad. Also great for dipping veggies!

10-12 cloves garlic
250ml/8fl oz flax oil or olive oil
125ml/4fl oz balsamic vinegar
125ml/4fl oz water

1 teaspoon salt
1/2 teaspoon pepper
1 tablespoon Dijon mustard

Separate (but don't peel) the cloves of garlic and roast in an un-oiled pan for 10-15 minutes at 180°C/350°F/gas mark 4, turning occasionally. Set aside and peel garlic when cool. In a blender or food processor, blend together the garlic, oil, vinegar, water, salt, pepper, and mustard until smooth.

# BALSAMIC MAPLE DRESSING

Sweet but tart, this dressing is easy to make.

125ml/4fl oz balsamic vinegar
2 tablespoons maple syrup

In a small bowl, whisk together the vinegar and syrup. Yum!

# GREEN GODDESS DRESSING

A colourful dressing with a superb flavour. This is excellent as a dip or dressing.

225g/8oz soft or medium tofu
4 tablespoons flax oil or olive oil
1/2 tablespoon chives
15g/1/2 oz fresh parsley
2 tablespoons vinegar

1/2 small onion
1-3 cloves garlic
1/8 teaspoon pepper
1/2 teaspoon salt

In a blender or food processor, blend together all the ingredients until smooth and creamy.

# CREAMY ITALIAN DRESSING

A cool, zesty version of this ever so popular dressing.

225g/8oz soft or medium tofu
125ml/4fl oz flax oil or olive oil
3 tablespoons vinegar
1 teaspoon salt
1/8 teaspoon pepper

4 cloves garlic, crushed
2 tablespoons sweet pickle or 1 large gherkin, chopped
1/4 teaspoon dried oregano
1/8 teaspoon red chilli flakes

In a blender or food processor, blend together the tofu, oil, vinegar, salt, and pepper until smooth and creamy. Fold in the garlic, relish, oregano, and red chilli flakes. Excellent as a tortilla chip dip in addition to a salad dressing.

# FABULOUS FRENCH DRESSING

A tangy dressing with superb flavour.

1 garlic clove, finely chopped
1/2 teaspoon salt
1/4 teaspoon mustard powder
1/4 teaspoon paprika

1/4 teaspoon pepper
4 tablespoons flax oil or olive oil
2 tablespoons vinegar

In a small bowl, whisk together all the ingredients. Serve over a nice green salad.

# THOUSAND ISLAND DRESSING

A creamy classic.

225g/8oz soft or medium tofu
125ml/4fl oz ketchup (pg. 152)
2 tablespoons flax oil or olive oil
1/2 small onion, finely chopped
1-2 cloves garlic, crushed

1/4 teaspoon salt
3 teaspoons sweet pickle
3 teaspoons green olives, finely chopped
6-8 sprigs parsley, chopped

In a blender or food processor, blend together the tofu, ketchup, oil, onions, garlic, and salt until smooth and creamy. Fold in the pickle, olives, and parsley.


# SWEET GINGER DRESSING

This sophisticated dressing lends its flavour to any vegetable it tops.

115g/4oz soft or medium tofu
2 tablespoons gomashio (pg. 154)
2 tablespoons sesame oil
4 tablespoons flax oil or olive oil
125ml/4fl oz rice vinegar

2 tablespoons maple syrup
1 tablespoon brown rice miso
1 clove garlic
1 1/2 tablespoons fresh ginger, grated
1/2 teaspoon pepper

In a blender or food processor, blend together all the ingredients until smooth and creamy.

# CAESAR SALAD DRESSING

Unique in flavour, this recipe is best when tossed with romaine lettuce and croutons (pg. 152).

75g/3oz soft or medium tofu

1½ teaspoons Dijon mustard

½ teaspoon kelp powder

2 tablespoons faux Parmesan cheese (pg. 154)

⅛ teaspoon sweetener

2 tablespoons lemon juice or vinegar

1 clove garlic, crushed

1 tablespoon flax oil or olive oil

¼ teaspoon salt

¼ teaspoon pepper

In a blender or food processor, blend together all the ingredients until smooth and creamy.

# SARAH'S QUICK & EASY SESAME DRESSING

Quick, hurry, let's eat! You can use this over a salad or in a noodle toss.

2 tablespoons sesame oil

4 tablespoons Braggs

4 tablespoons rice vinegar

Whisk together all the ingredients.

# JANA'S FAMOUS HERB DRESSING

Toss this dressing over Jana's Garden Kitchen Salad (pg.61) and thank your lucky stars we introduced you to her! You could also use it as a topping for rice.

4 tablespoons flax oil
4 tablespoons nutritional yeast flakes
4 tablespoons cider vinegar
2 teaspoons pepper
2 tablespoons maple syrup

2 cloves garlic, chopped
2 tablespoons fresh thyme, chopped
1 tablespoon fresh rosemary, chopped
1 teaspoon fresh oregano, diced
1 tablespoon sesame seeds or gomashio (pg. 154)

In a small bowl, whisk together all the ingredients. Stir well before serving.

# NICE 'N SPICY AVOCADO DRESSING

This creamy dressing goes great over a fresh green salad or can be used as a veggie dip.

1 avocado
1 tablespoon lemon juice or vinegar
125ml/4fl oz faux sour cream (pg. 152)
5 tablespoons flax oil or olive oil

1 clove garlic, crushed
1/2 teaspoon chilli powder
1/4 teaspoon salt
1/4 teaspoon Tabasco or other hot sauce

In a blender or food processor, blend together all the ingredients until smooth and creamy.

# VEGAN SAUCES & SPREADS

# SAUCES

Sauces can complement a variety of dishes and grains by adding savoury flavours and zest while at the same time providing the body with necessary vitamins and minerals. With these recipes, you can be sure that they will not only add a nutritional note, but will please your palate, too.

# MIGHTY MISO GRAVY

This recipe is an addictive topping that partners well with savoury biscuits (pg. 116) or pan-fried potatoes (pg. 41). Use your imagination and discover a dish of your own to use with this delectable sauce.

6-10 mushrooms, chopped
1 medium onion, chopped
1 tablespoon olive oil
2-3 tablespoons Braggs or soy sauce
cayenne pepper (to taste)
dried basil (to taste)

dried dill (to taste)
pepper (to taste)
40-50g/1 1/2-2oz flour
300ml/1/2 pint vegetable stock or water
1 teaspoon miso

In a medium saucepan, sauté the mushrooms and onions in oil on medium-high heat until onions are translucent and mushrooms are tender. Add the Braggs, cayenne, basil, dill, and pepper and stir together. Remove from heat and slowly stir in the flour, mixing together well. It will become pasty and dry. Slowly start adding the stock a little at a time until everything becomes well mixed and there are no lumps. Place back onto medium heat and simmer until sauce is thickened, stirring often. At the last minute, stir in miso and serve. **Makes 4-6 servings.**

# EAZY BREEZY CHEEZY SAUCE

A delicious, versatile, and cheesy sauce to serve over burritos, pasta, burgers, or veggies — anything you can think of, really!

40g/1 1/2 oz nutritional yeast
3 tablespoons flour
4 teaspoons arrowroot powder or cornflour
1/2 teaspoon salt

250ml/8fl oz water
1 tablespoon olive oil
2 teaspoons Dijon mustard

In a small saucepan, whisk together the yeast, flour, arrowroot powder, and salt. Add the water and oil and continue to whisk thoroughly. Stir over medium heat until sauce becomes thick, then stir in the mustard. Heat for 30 seconds more and serve. **Makes 2-4 servings.**

# PERFECT PESTO

These next two pesto recipes are delicious favourites that will linger in the hearts and minds of those who try them. Whip up these fabulous sauces and team them with pasta, rice, or veggies.

90g/3 1/2 oz fresh basil, chopped
40g/1 1/2 oz fresh parsley, chopped
2 tablespoons soy Parmesan cheese
3 cloves garlic, crushed

2 tablespoons pine nuts, toasted
3 teaspoons miso
4-5 tablespoons water

In a blender or food processor, blend together the basil, parsley, Parmesan, garlic, nuts, and miso until well combined. With the machine running, slowly add water until you've reach the desired consistency. Heat and serve over pasta or rice, or use in place of tomato sauce on pizza. **Makes 2-4 servings.**

# ZESTY TOMATO PESTO

4 medium tomatoes, chopped
1 bunch spinach, chopped
40g/1 1/2 oz spring onions, chopped
125ml/4fl oz olive oil

4 cloves garlic, crushed
4-5 teaspoons fresh basil, chopped
salt (to taste)

In a blender or food processor, blend together the tomatoes, spinach, onions, oil, garlic, and basil until you've reached the desired consistency. Add salt to taste. Heat and serve over pasta or rice, or use in place of tomato sauce on pizza. **Makes 2-4 servings.**

# SUPER EASY TOMATO SAUCE

Great for pizza or when you're in a hurry.

2 tablespoons olive oil
1/2 medium onion, chopped
2 cloves garlic, crushed
3 tablespoons tomato purée
1 medium or large tomato, diced

1/2 teaspoon dried basil
1/2 teaspoon dried oregano
1/2 teaspoon salt
1/2 teaspoon pepper

In blender or food processor, blend together all the ingredients until you've reached the desired consistency. Use immediately. **Makes 250ml/8fl oz.**

# TRADITIONAL TOMATO SAUCE

Here's a dilly of a sauce that will make Mama weep because she knows it's better than hers.

4 cloves garlic, crushed
1 small onion, chopped
1 small carrot, chopped
175g/6oz mixed green and red pepper, chopped
8-10 mushrooms, sliced
1 teaspoon dried oregano
1/4 teaspoon dried basil
1/4 teaspoon dried thyme

1/4 teaspoon pepper
1 teaspoon salt
2 tablespoons olive oil
1 teaspoon sweetener
1 x165g/51/2oz can tomato purée
5-8 fresh tomatoes, diced
2 x 400g cans chopped tomatoes

In a large pan, sauté the garlic, onions, carrots, peppers, mushrooms, oregano, basil, thyme, pepper, and salt in oil on medium heat until onions are translucent. Add sweetener, tomato purée and tomatoes. Cover with lid and simmer on medium-low heat for 15-30 minutes, stirring occasionally. Serve with pasta or use for lasagne (pg. 101). This sauce freezes well. Note: this sauce is thick; if you like a thinner sauce, add a little stock or water until you've reach the desired consistency. **Makes 4-6 servings.**

# GERRY'S SAUCY CREAMY SAUCE

My Gerry makes a mean cream sauce. He's so saucy! **S**

5-8 cloves garlic, crushed
8-10 mushrooms, chopped
1 tablespoon olive oil
125ml/4fl oz coconut milk (soy milk works, but not as well)

3 tablespoons soy Parmesan cheese
1/4 teaspoon nutmeg
1/2-1 teaspoon pepper

In a medium saucepan, sauté the garlic and mushrooms in oil on medium-low heat, ensuring the garlic doesn't burn. In a small pan, bring the coconut milk to a boil on medium-high heat. When it starts to bubble, add the Parmesan, nutmeg, and pepper and remove from heat. Whisk until smooth and the cheese has melted.

Pour this mixture into the saucepan with the mushrooms and stir together. Simmer on medium-high heat to reduce the liquid by half. Be careful not to burn it! Stir constantly. Once it reaches the desired consistency, pour over pasta or rice and serve. **Makes 2-4 servings.**

# GINGER PEANUT SAUCE

This sure hit, containing a lovely combination of flavours such as ginger, sesame oil, curry, and peanuts, is not only just for stir-fries, but is great with any pasta dish.

1 medium onion, chopped
4 cloves garlic, crushed
1 tablespoon olive oil
250ml/8fl oz hot water
1/2 teaspoon curry powder

1 tablespoon fresh ginger, grated
225g/8oz natural peanut butter (or other nut butter)
3 tablespoons Braggs or soy sauce
1 tablespoon sesame oil
dash of cayenne pepper

In a medium saucepan, sauté the onions and garlic in oil until onions are translucent. Stir in the water, curry powder, ginger, nut butter, Braggs, sesame oil, and cayenne pepper. Whisk or stir together until smooth. Simmer for 5-7 minutes on medium-high heat, stirring often. Serve over noodles, stir-fries, or vegetables. **Makes 2-4 servings.**

# SPICY GARLIC TOSS FOR NOODLES

A simple sauce that overflows with flavour. A light but lively toss to spark up your noodles.

4-6 cloves garlic, crushed
2 tablespoons olive oil
4 tablespoons water
2 teaspoons Braggs or soy sauce
1/2 teaspoon paprika

1/4 teaspoon dried basil
1/4 teaspoon dried thyme
1/4 teaspoon dried pepper
1/4 teaspoon salt
dash of cayenne pepper

In a small saucepan, sauté garlic in 1 tablespoon of oil on medium-low heat until garlic is translucent. Be careful not to burn. Add the water, remaining oil, Braggs, paprika, basil, thyme, pepper, salt, and cayenne and bring to a boil. Simmer for 8-15 minutes. Toss with soba or buckwheat noodles. Serve the noodles with steamed veggies and tofu or eat noodles on their own, right out of the pan, for that bachelor look. **Makes 2-4 servings.**

# FESTIVE CRANBERRY SAUCE

This seductive red sauce will impress and delight your guests come harvest time when presented alongside the tofu turkey (pg.110). Other possibilities include a topping for vanilla banana ice cream (pg. 148) or chocolate "cheese" cake (pg. 139).

175g/6oz fresh or frozen (thawed) cranberries
250ml/8fl oz maple syrup
250ml/8fl oz cranberry juice

grated zest of orange
115g/4oz walnuts, chopped (optional)

In a medium saucepan, bring the cranberries, maple syrup, cranberry juice, and orange zest to a boil. Lower heat to medium and simmer for 10 minutes or until the cranberries pop open. Skim off any foam that forms on the surface. Stir in optional walnuts. Chill before using. **Makes 4-6 servings.**

# SPREADS

Spreads can complement sandwiches by adding savoury flavours and zest while at the same time providing the body with necessary nutrients.

# EASY GARLIC SPREAD

Relish this spread not only because it's effortless to prepare, but it can be served on a variety of breads or crackers to accompany any salad, soup, or entrée. As you may know, cooked garlic has the strongest aroma of any member of the onion family member. Be sure to have some fresh parsley nearby to chew on in order to curb any nasty garlic breath.

125ml/4fl oz olive oil
6-10 cloves garlic, crushed

1/2 small onion, finely chopped
1/8 teaspoon salt

In a blender or food processor, blend all the ingredients together. Spread over bread slices and wrap bread in foil and bake at 180°C/350°F/gas mark 4 for 15-25 minutes.
**Makes approx. 175ml/6fl oz.**

# FANCY GARLIC SPREAD

This spread is a good companion with crackers, bread, or whatever makes you happy.

1 small red onion, chopped
6-10 cloves garlic, crushed
3 1/2 tablespoons olive oil
1/2 tablespoon balsamic vinegar

2 1/2 tablespoons fresh thyme
salt (to taste)
pepper (to taste)

In a medium saucepan, sauté the onions and garlic in 1 1/2 tablespoons of the oil on medium-low heat until onions are translucent. In a blender or food processor, blend together the onion mixture, vinegar, thyme, salt, and pepper and remaining oil. **Makes approx. 125ml/4fl oz.**

# EASY VEGGIE BUTTER

This butter recipe is so easy to prepare, it's a must in all vegan kitchens. It's perfect on toast, muffins, potatoes — whatever butter is good on.

175g/6oz soft tofu
2 tablespoons flax oil or olive oil

pinch of salt
dash of turmeric

In blender or food processor, blend together all the ingredients until well mixed. Store in sealable container. Will keep in the fridge for 4-7 days. **Makes approx. 250ml/8fl oz.**

# STEPHANIE'S YUMMY VEGGIE SPREAD

This veggie spread is to die for! Use in sandwiches or wherever a delicious spread is needed.

125ml/4fl oz veggie butter (above) (or margarine)
3 tablespoons tomato purée
2 cloves garlic, crushed
1 teaspoon dried oregano
1 teaspoon dried dill

1/2 teaspoon dried basil
1 tablespoon fresh parsley
1/2 small green pepper, chopped
1-2 spring onions, chopped

In a blender or food processor, blend together the veggie butter, tomato purée, garlic, oregano, dill, basil, and parsley. Pour into a bowl and add the chopped pepper and onion. Stir together and place in sealable container. This butter will keep in the fridge for 7-10 days. **Makes approx. 175ml/6fl oz.**

# ELEGANT CREAM CHEESE

A nutritious, vegan version of the popular basic cream cheese spread. The velvety smooth texture will make you want to try the following three variations too.

225g/8oz soft or medium tofu
25g/1oz cashew pieces
2 teaspoons sweetener

1-2 tablespoons water
1 teaspoon salt
1/2 teaspoon pepper

In a blender or food processor, blend together all the ingredients until smooth and thick. Place in sealable container. Will keep in the fridge for 4-7 days. **Makes approx. 250ml/8fl oz.**


# GARLIC DILL CREAM CHEESE

The garlic combined with the dill gives this tofu cream cheese a perky flavour.

225g/8oz soft or medium tofu
25g/1oz cashew pieces
2 teaspoons sweetener
2-5 cloves garlic, crushed

1-2 tablespoons water
1 teaspoon salt
1/2 teaspoon pepper
1 tablespoon dried dill

In a blender or food processor, blend together all the ingredients until smooth and thick. Place in sealable container. Will keep in the fridge for 4-7 days. **Makes approx. 250ml/8fl oz.**


# SPRING ONION CREAM CHEESE

The onions make for a colourful spread and a subtle flavour.

225g/8oz soft or medium tofu
25g/1oz cashew pieces
2 teaspoons sweetener
1-2 tablespoons water

1 teaspoon salt
1/2 teaspoon pepper
4-6 spring onions chopped

In a blender or food processor, blend together all the ingredients until smooth and thick. Place in sealable container. Will keep in the fridge for 4-7 days. **Makes approx. 250ml/8fl oz.**

# TO-FRUITY CREAM CHEESE

A refreshing fruit-filled version of a classic favourite.

225g/8oz soft or medium tofu
25g/1oz cashew pieces
4 teaspoons sweetener

1/2 teaspoon salt
50g/2oz fruit (e.g., strawberries, blueberries)

In a blender or food processor, blend together all the ingredients until smooth and thick. Place in sealable container. Will keep in the fridge for 4-7 days. **Makes approx. 250ml/8fl oz.**

# SUNFLOWER SEED AVOCADO SPREAD

This rich spread is delicious, nutritious, and a snap to make. The avocado ensures a smooth and creamy texture while providing the body with such good things as fibre, vitamin C, and vitamin E. The fat found in avocados is monounsaturated and is believed to be a beneficial fat.

65g/2 1/2 oz raw sunflower seeds
4 tablespoons soy milk
4 tablespoons tahini
1 avocado
1/2 teaspoon turmeric

1/4 teaspoon mustard seeds
1/2 teaspoon pepper
1/4 teaspoon salt
1 teaspoon lemon juice

In a blender or food processor, blend together all the ingredients until smooth and thick. Place in sealable container. Will keep in the fridge for 4-7 days. **Makes approx. 250ml/8fl oz.**

# SUN SEED SANDWICH SPREAD

What could satisfy any sandwich more than being smothered with a deliciously seedy sandwich spread?

175g/6oz sunflower seeds, toasted
2 tablespoons sesame seeds, toasted
3 tablespoons flax oil or olive oil
1-2 cloves garlic, crushed
2 tablespoons grated soy cheese

1 tablespoon light miso
1 tablespoon Braggs or soy sauce
1 stalk celery, diced
1 tomato, roughly chopped
pepper (to taste)

Toast the sunflower and sesame seeds in an oven at 160°C/325°C/gas mark 3 for 7-10 minutes. In a blender or food processor, coarsely grind 150g/5oz of the sunflower seeds. Add the oil, garlic, cheese, miso, Braggs, celery, tomatoes, and pepper and blend until you reach desired consistency. Mix in the sesame seeds and remaining sunflower seeds. Store in sealable container. Use as sandwich spread or on crackers. **Makes approx. 350ml/12fl oz.**

# ZESTY CHEESE SPREAD

The sautéed red pepper gives this spread a robust flavour. Red peppers, being high in vitamin C, are a perfect partner for the iron-packed sesame seeds. The combination of these two ingredients is beneficial because iron is absorbed more efficiently when vitamin C is present.

1 small red pepper, chopped
1 tablespoon olive oil
175g/6oz cashews
50g/2oz sesame seeds
125ml/4fl oz water

65g/2¹/2 oz nutritional yeast flakes
4 tablespoons lemon juice or vinegar
4 tablespoons flax oil
1 tablespoon Braggs or soy sauce

In a small saucepan, sauté the peppers in the oil on medium heat until soft. In a blender or food processor, blend the sautéed peppers, cashews, sesame seeds, water, yeast, lemon juice, flax oil, and Braggs until smooth. Place in sealable container. Will keep in the fridge for 7-10 days. Serve on bread, crackers, celery, or mixed into hot rice. **Makes approx. 250ml/8fl oz.**

# OI-VEY! MOCK CHOPPED LIVER

This spread is best served over matzo.

90g/3¹/2oz mushrooms, roughly chopped
1 large onion, roughly chopped
1 tablespoon olive oil

50g/2oz walnuts
¹/2 teaspoon salt
¹/2 teaspoon pepper

In a medium saucepan, sauté the mushrooms and onions in oil on medium heat until onions become translucent. In a blender or food processor, chop the walnuts and add the mushroom/onion mixture and salt and pepper. Blend together for 30 seconds. Serve chilled. **Makes approx. 175ml/6fl oz.**

# VEGAN
# SIDE DISHES

This section includes mouthwatering recipes that can be served as appetizers, with an accompanying side dish, or teamed up with a main dish. Any way you choose to serve them, they are guaranteed to please.

# HOLY MOLY HUMMUS

Savour this creamy, smooth Mediterranean dip made from chickpeas, one of the most nutritious beans of all, and garlic, known for its medicinal properties and lovely scent. A snap to make, it can be a fantastic accompaniment for your favourite vegetables, crackers, tortilla chips, or bread. You can alter the taste of this recipe by changing the beans. Try black beans and sun-dried tomatoes for a treat. Check out the kids' version of hummus on pg. 170.

1 small onion, chopped
5 cloves garlic (more if you dare), crushed
splash of olive oil
350g/12oz cooked or canned chickpeas
175ml/6fl oz tahini
1 1/2 tablespoons Braggs or soy sauce
125ml/4fl oz lemon juice or 4 tablespoons water
   plus 4 tablespoons cider vinegar

15g/1/2 oz fresh parsley, chopped
2 tablespoons chopped jalapeño chilli (optional)
1 teaspoon cumin
1/4 teaspoon cayenne pepper
1 teaspoon salt

In a small saucepan, sauté onions and garlic in a splash of oil on medium heat until onions are translucent. In a blender or food processor, blend the sautéed onions, chickpeas, tahini, Braggs, lemon juice, parsley, jalapeño, cumin, cayenne, and salt until you reach the desired consistency. **Makes approx. 475ml/16fl oz.**

# GORGEOUS GUACAMOLE

A smooth, silky, scrumptious, and spicy spread.

3 avocados
4 tablespoons lime juice
1 medium tomato, chopped
1-2 cloves garlic, crushed

1-2 jalapeño chillies, seeded and chopped
1/2 hot pepper, chopped (optional)
1/2 red onion, chopped
1 teaspoon pepper

Scoop out avocados into a medium bowl. Add lime juice and mash together with a fork. Add the tomatoes, garlic, jalapeño and peppers, onions, and pepper. Stir together. **Makes approx. 350ml/12fl oz.**

# FRESH TOMATO SALSA

Enjoy these three deliciously spiced, addictive salsas. These are essential dips for corn chips; they also make great toppings for burgers, burritos, or even on top of a salad instead of dressing. Luckily, the following recipes are no bother to whip up.

4-6 medium tomatoes, chopped

2-4 cloves garlic

3-6 sprigs coriander

3 sprigs parsley

1 tablespoon red wine vinegar

1 tablespoon flax oil

2-4 hot chillies (you decide the heat)

1 x 175g/6oz  can tomato purée

1/2 red onion, chopped

50g/2oz olives, chopped (optional)

1 teaspoon paprika (optional)

In a blender or food processor, blend the tomatoes, garlic, coriander, parsley, vinegar, oil, peppers, and tomato purée until well mixed. Spoon into a small bowl and add onions, olives, and paprika, and stir well. **Makes approx. 475ml/16fl oz.**

# BEN'S BLACK BEAN SALSA

300g/11oz cooked or canned black beans

1-2 jalapeño chillies, seeded and finely chopped

2-3 medium tomatoes, chopped

1 avocado, chopped

175g/6oz sweetcorn kernels

1/2 red pepper, chopped

1/2 yellow pepper, chopped

1-3 tablespoons lime juice

1 clove garlic, crushed

3-6 sprigs coriander, finely chopped

salt (to taste)

In a medium bowl, stir together the beans, jalapeños, tomatoes, avocado, sweetcorn, peppers, lime juice, garlic, and coriander. Add salt to taste. **Makes approx. 475ml/16fl oz.**

# SWEET GINGER-BLACK BEAN SALSA

150g/5oz cooked or canned black beans

1/2 medium red pepper, roughly chopped

1 jalapeño chilli, roughly chopped

1/2 small red onion, roughly chopped

2 tablespoons lime juice

2 tablespoons garlic-chilli flax oil

1 teaspoon fresh ginger, roughly chopped

1/2 teaspoon sweetener

1/2 teaspoon salt

4-6 sprigs coriander

In a blender or food processor, blend three-quarters of the beans, red pepper and jalapeño chilli, onion, lime juice, oil, ginger, sweetener, salt, and coriander. Blend on high until well mixed. Pour into a serving bowl and add the remaining beans. Stir together. **Makes approx. 475ml/16fl oz.**

# SPINACH & ARTICHOKE DIP

Combine iron-packed spinach with the unique flavour of artichokes to create this elegant dip. This dish will impress the most gourmet of diners at your next soirée. Serve with tortilla chips, crackers, or pitta bread.

25g/1oz fresh spinach
75g/3oz soy Parmesan cheese
225g/8oz marinated artichoke hearts, drained
1/4 teaspoon pepper

1 teaspoon lemon juice
115g/4oz grated soy mozzarella cheese

Preheat oven to 180°C/350°F/gas mark 4. In a blender or food processor, blend the spinach, 50g/2oz of Parmesan, artichokes, pepper, lemon juice, and mozzarella until well mixed. Spoon into a lightly oiled casserole dish and top with the remaining Parmesan. Cover and bake for 20 minutes, until hot and bubbly. Remove from the oven and let sit 5 minutes before serving. **Makes 4–6 servings.**

# JB'S SWEET DILL CARROTS

In order for JB to lend his name to any recipe, it must first reach the highest criteria of sweetness, oranginess, and dill-ectability. These carrots have achieved the highest stature in all of these criteria.

6-10 medium carrots, sliced
1 tablespoon dried dill

1 tablespoon sweetener
1 tablespoon margarine, flax oil, or olive oil

In a medium pan or a steamer, steam the carrots until they can be pierced easily with a fork. Place the carrots in a small bowl and add the rest of the ingredients. Stir together until well incorporated. **Makes 2-4 servings.**

# JANA'S HONEY LEMON CARROTS

This side dish is a lovely complement to Jana's Healthy Rice (pg. 107).

125ml/4fl oz water
5 medium carrots, sliced
1/4 teaspoon lemon juice
2 tablespoons maple syrup

2 tablespoons fresh rosemary, chopped
1 teaspoon salt
1 teaspoon pepper

In a medium saucepan, bring the water to a boil. Add the carrots and simmer until carrots are almost cooked. Stir in the lemon juice, honey, rosemary, salt, and pepper and simmer on low heat for 5 more minutes. **Makes 2-4 servings.**

# ROASTED GARLIC POTATOES

These tasty spuds, spiced with garden herbs, will feel right at home alongside breakfast, lunch, or dinner entrées.

4-5 medium potatoes, cubed
2 tablespoons olive oil
8 cloves garlic, crushed
2 teaspoons sage

2 tablespoons rosemary
1/2 teaspoon salt
1 teaspoon pepper

Preheat oven to 200°C/400°F/gas mark 6. Place the cubed potatoes in a medium bowl and add the rest of the ingredients and stir together. Lay evenly onto a baking sheet or roasting tin and bake in the oven for 30-40 minutes, until potatoes are golden brown and can be easily pierced with a fork. **Makes 4-6 servings.**

# MASHED GARLIC POTATOES WITH KALE

Easy to make and delicious to taste. This side dish is sure to be a hit.

3-4 medium potatoes, roughly chopped
1 medium onion, chopped
4 cloves garlic, crushed
2 tablespoons olive oil
4-5 stalks kale, chopped

125ml/4fl oz soy milk
2 tablespoons flax oil
2 tablespoons Braggs
pepper (to taste)

In a large pan of water, boil the potatoes until they can be pierced easily with a fork. In a medium saucepan, sauté the onions and garlic in the oil on medium heat until the onion becomes translucent. Add the kale and cover pan with lid. Lower heat and simmer for 5-10 minutes until kale becomes soft. Set aside. When potatoes are ready, drain and place them in a large bowl. Mash together with milk, flax oil, Braggs, and pepper. Stir in the kale mixture and mix together well. **Makes 4-6 servings.**

# TANYA'S SWEET MASH

This mashed delight adds glamour, diversity, and colour to the often-repetitive list of potato dishes. Surprise your guests with a sweet version of a classic favourite.

1 large kuri (onion) squash, peeled and quartered
2 medium potatoes, roughly chopped
2 cloves garlic, crushed

1 small onion, chopped
2 tablespoons Braggs or soy sauce
2 tablespoons flax oil

In a medium pan of water, boil the squash, potatoes, garlic, and onions until you can pierce the squash and potatoes easily with a fork. Drain the water, then add the Braggs and oil to the pan. Mash together until you reach the desired consistency. **Makes 4-6 servings.**

# DIJON SCALLOPED POTATOES

The rich and flavourful seasoning of this recipe will make leftovers a thing of the past. The addition of the spicy Dijon mustard will delight sophisticated palates.

1 medium onion, chopped
1 teaspoon turmeric
2 1/2 tablespoons olive oil
40g/1 1/2 oz flour
125ml/4fl oz vegetable stock or water
4 tablespoons Dijon mustard

475ml/16fl oz soy milk
1/2 teaspoon salt
1/8 teaspoon pepper
1 teaspoon Braggs or soy sauce
3-6 spring onions, chopped
6 medium potatoes, sliced into coins

Preheat oven to 190°C/375°F/gas mark 5. In a medium saucepan, sauté the onions and turmeric in oil on medium-high heat until the onions are translucent. Mix in the flour, stirring constantly for about 2 minutes, resulting in a dry mixture. Slowly stir in stock, mustard, milk, salt, pepper, Braggs, and spring onions. Stir until well mixed and there are no flour lumps. Set aside. Place sliced potatoes into a lightly oiled 23x33cm/9x13in baking tray. Pour the sauce over the potatoes and bake uncovered for 45-60 minutes. **Makes 4-6 servings.**

# VEGETABLE MEDLEY KUGEL

Kugel is a Jewish baked pudding that can be made out of just about anything – fruit, potatoes, noodles – whatever. Complete the menu with this unique dish, a delightful medley of vegetables and matzo.

4 matzos
350g/12oz courgettes, chopped
2 medium carrots, chopped
5-8 mushrooms, chopped
115g/4oz broccoli, chopped
1 small onion, finely chopped

splash of olive oil
125ml/4fl oz vegetable stock or water
egg replacer (to equal 2 eggs)
1/2 teaspoon salt
1/2 teaspoon pepper

Preheat oven to 190°C/375°F/gas mark 5. Break matzos into quarters and soak in a bowl of water until soft. Drain, but do not squeeze dry. In a medium saucepan, sauté the courgettes, carrots, mushrooms, broccoli, and onions in a splash of oil on medium-high heat until carrots are tender. Place the vegetables in a large casserole dish and add the stock, egg replacer, salt, and pepper, and mix thoroughly. Stir in the matzo, and bake for 20 minutes. **Makes 2-4 servings.**

# SWEET POTATO & APPLE KUGEL

A tempting dish that will delight all who consume it.

675g/1 1/2 lb sweet potatoes or yams, peeled and
    finely chopped
2 green apples, cored and thinly sliced
90g/3oz raisins

250ml/8fl oz apple juice or water
1 teaspoon cinnamon
50g/2oz matzo meal or breadcrumbs
50g/2oz walnuts (optional)

Preheat oven to 190°C/375°F/gas mark 5. In a large casserole dish, mix together all the ingredients. Bake uncovered for 45-50 minutes. **Makes 4-6 servings.**

# RUSTIC ROASTED VEGGIES

These bite-sized morsels are so savoury and juicy they will explode in your mouth. Roasting them adds a depth and richness that transforms ordinary cooked vegetables into something elegant.

2-4 medium carrots, chopped
2-3 medium potatoes, chopped
8-10 cloves garlic, peeled
6-8 mushrooms, halved
1 small yam, cubed
(plus any other vegetables you want)
225g/8oz medium tofu, cubed

2-4 tablespoons olive oil
1 tablespoon dill
2 tablespoons rosemary
crushed chillies (to taste)
salt (to taste)
pepper (to taste)

Preheat oven to 180°C/350°F/gas mark 4. Place the vegetables and tofu on lightly oiled baking sheet or roasting tin and drizzle the oil over them. Sprinkle with dill, rosemary, chillies, salt, and pepper and mix together until well incorporated. Bake for 40-60 minutes, stirring every 10 minutes. Remove from oven when potatoes can be pierced easily with a fork. **Makes 4-6 servings.**

# VEGETABLE RICE PILAF

Adding this simply scrumptious rice to sautéed vegetables makes a dish that is sure to please. For variety, use quinoa instead of rice. Quinoa takes half the amount of time to cook and has an interesting nutty flavour.

400g/14oz brown rice
1 litre/1¾ pints water
½ teaspoon turmeric
2-4 cloves garlic, chopped
1 small onion, diced
1 medium carrot, diced
½ medium red pepper, diced

½ medium green pepper, diced
1 teaspoon salt
1 tablespoon olive oil
115g/4oz peas
15g/½ oz fresh parsley or 2 tablespoons dried
  parsley

In a medium pan with a tight-fitting lid, bring rice, water, and turmeric to a boil. Lower heat and simmer for 40 minutes or until rice is done. While the rice is cooking, in a medium saucepan, sauté the garlic, onions, carrots, peppers, and salt in the oil on medium-high heat for 5-7 minutes. Add the peas and parsley and simmer for 5 minutes more, then set aside in a large bowl. When the rice is cooked, add it to the vegetables and stir together. **Makes 4-6 servings.**

# VORACIOUS VEGAN PÂTÉ

I really enjoy this recipe. It's a versatile, tasty spread that can be served with crackers or bread, or done up sandwich-style. If you're really feeling dangerous, spice things up by throwing in a habanero chilli! **T**

2 medium onions, diced
5 mushrooms, diced
4 cloves garlic, diced
splash of olive oil
150g/5oz raw sunflower seeds, ground
50g/2oz flour
40g/1½ oz nutritional yeast
2 teaspoons dried basil
1 teaspoon salt

1 teaspoon dried thyme
½ teaspoon dried sage
50g/2oz kelp powder
350ml/12fl oz water
3 tablespoons Braggs or soy sauce
225g/8oz potatoes, grated
5 tablespoons olive oil
1 habanero chilli, seeded and finely chopped (optional)

Preheat oven to 180°C/350°F/gas mark 4. In a medium saucepan, sauté the onions, mushrooms, and garlic in oil on medium-high heat until tender. Meanwhile, in a large bowl, combine the ground sunflower seeds (you can grind them in a blender or a food processor), flour, yeast, basil, salt, thyme, sage, and kelp. Add the water, Braggs, potatoes, and oil and stir together. Stir in the sautéed vegetables and optional pepper and mix well. Spoon mixture into a lightly oiled 23cm/9in pie plate. Bake for 45 minutes or until centre is set and browned. Chill thoroughly before serving.
**Makes 4-6 servings.**

# BRILLIANT BAKED BEANS

Beans are an important part of our daily nutritional requirements. The food guide states you should consume 2 servings daily or have them make up 5 to 15 per cent of your diet. This bean bake is a savoury, satisfying way to meet your bean quota for the day.

300g/11oz cooked or canned beans (e.g., pinto, kidney, haricot, or soy)
350ml/12fl oz vegetable stock
1 teaspoon molasses
1 x 175g/6oz can tomato purée
1 small onion, chopped

1-2 cloves garlic, crushed
4 tablespoons Braggs or soy sauce
1 tablespoon mustard powder
1 teaspoon cumin
1/2 teaspoon paprika

Preheat oven to 180°C/350°F/gas mark 4. In a large baking dish, stir all the ingredients together. Bake uncovered for 40 minutes. **Makes 2-4 servings.**

# LARRY'S RE-FRIED BEANS

Our friend Larry thinks he knows everything there is to know. Well, he sure knows his beans.

275g/10oz cooked or canned beans (e.g., pinto, kidney, black)
125ml/4fl oz vegetable stock or water
2 cloves garlic, crushed

25g/1oz coriander, chopped
1 teaspoon cumin
1/4 teaspoon cayenne pepper
1 plum tomato, sliced

In a medium pan, cook all the ingredients on medium heat for 10-15 minutes, stirring occasionally. Remove from heat. Mash with a fork and serve as is over rice, or in items such as burritos (pg.99). **Makes 2-4 servings.**

# VEGAN
# MAIN DISHES

Main dishes are the focus of all dinner tables. Many people can't imagine a main meal without the presence of a meat dish. These exciting vegan recipes offer nutritious alternatives to that old-fashioned idea. We hope you will be inspired to use vegetables, herbs, and other delicious ingredients in many different new ways. There are both light and filling main dishes here to expand your culinary skills in a healthy direction.

# SARAH'S DELICIOUS CHILLI

This is one of my favourite recipes. You can whip this up in an instant and feed the masses at a moment's notice! This chilli always tastes best the next day and freezes well. **S**

1 medium onion, chopped
2 medium carrots, chopped
1 tablespoon olive oil
450g/1lb cooked or canned kidney beans
2 x 400g cans chopped tomatoes
175g/6oz tomato purée
350g/12oz cooked or canned chickpeas

8-12 mushrooms, chopped
350g can sweetcorn
150g/5oz rice
1-3 tablespoons chilli powder
1 tablespoon pepper
2 tablespoons curry paste
475ml/16fl oz vegetable stock or water

In a large pot, sauté the onions and carrots in oil on medium-high heat until the onions become translucent. Add the remaining ingredients and stir together. Simmer on medium-low heat for 40-60 minutes, stirring occasionally. Serve with fresh bread. Note: you could also add any other veggies you have kicking around; peppers or courgettes work well. **Makes 6-8 servings.**

# TANYA'S ASIAN CREATION

When I was living in Japan, I discovered the art of subtlety in cooking. I used my imagination and came up with masterpieces like this one using only salt and pepper as the spices. I had a hard time in Japan trying to adhere to my vegan lifestyle, but I stuck to my guns and I'm a better vegan warrior for it now. Enjoy this one. If you find it's a little too hot, you can use a little less pepper next time; my feelings won't be hurt. **T**

buckwheat noodles (enough for 4 people)
350g/12oz cubed squash (e.g., onion, kabocha,
    butternut or acorn; don't use spaghetti squash)
2 tablespoons olive oil
450g/1lb medium tofu, cubed
1-3 teaspoons pepper

1 teaspoon salt
3 spring onions, chopped
4 tablespoons flax oil
Braggs (garnish)
gomashio (pg.154) (garnish)

In a medium pan, boil the noodles in water on high heat. Meanwhile, in a medium saucepan, sauté the squash in the oil on high heat for about 5 minutes, then add the tofu, pepper, and salt. Continue cooking until the squash can be easily pierced with a fork. Add the onions, cover and set aside. When the noodles have finished cooking, rinse in hot water, then place back into the pot and toss with the flax oil to prevent the noodles from sticking. Place them into a bowl or on a plate and top with the squash mixture, then garnish with Braggs and gomashio. **Makes 2-4 servings.**

# RICE PAPER VEGGIE WRAPS

Light, refreshing, and easy to make. Excellent for picnics or hot summer days when cooking seems impossible.

4-6 mushrooms, chopped
125ml/4fl oz Braggs or soy sauce
1 large carrot, grated
4 radishes, grated
175g/6oz cabbage, grated

2 spring onions, chopped
1 medium tomato, chopped
115g/4oz sunflower sprouts
115g/4oz hummus (pg. 85)
6 sheets of rice paper

In a small bowl, marinate the mushrooms in the Braggs for 10-15 minutes. While marinating, prepare the remaining vegetables and set aside. Fill a large bowl with lukewarm water and soak 1 sheet of rice paper until paper becomes soft and pliable. Shake carefully or pat off excess water. Lay the sheet down on a plate or cutting board and fill the centre with a little bit of each vegetable, including the mushrooms, and about 2 tablespoons of hummus. Wrap up by folding up bottom edge, then fold in each side and lay seam-side down on plate. Repeat process. Use the remaining marinade as a dip. **Makes 6 wraps.**

# NORI SUSHI ROLLS

We're going to have a sushi party tonight! Alright!

400g/14oz cooked brown rice or sushi rice
2 tablespoons gomashio (pg. 154)
1 tablespoon maple syrup
1 tablespoon cider vinegar
150g/5oz carrot, grated
150g/5oz beetroot, grated
1 small cucumber, sliced like matchsticks

175g/6oz sprouts (e.g., sunflower, broccoli, spicy)
2-3 avocados, sliced
3 spring onions, chopped
8 nori sushi sheets
Braggs (for dipping)
wasabi (for dipping)

In a large bowl, combine the cooked rice, gomashio, maple syrup, and vinegar and place in refrigerator to chill for 10-15 minutes. When rice has chilled, place nori sheet on a sushi mat or cutting board and spread 1/8 of the rice mixture over 2/3 of the nori sheet closest to yourself. Add each vegetable, placing it in the middle of the rice mixture. Roll the nori away from you. Dab a little water with your finger to seal up the edges. Slice into two or four pieces. Use Braggs and wasabi for dipping. Try different sorts of vegetable combinations for variation. **Makes 16-32 rolls**.

# SWEET POLENTA PIE

This mouth-watering dish is just one example of how satisfying a masterful blend of roasted vegetables over a colourful bed of polenta can be. It will delight and excite your tastebuds.

**Roasted Veggie Topping:**

1 medium carrot, chopped
1 small courgette, chopped
4 mushrooms, quartered
1 small green pepper, sliced
1 small red pepper, sliced
1 small red onion, chopped
2 cloves garlic, crushed
125ml/4fl oz water

1 1/2 tablespoons tomato purée
1 teaspoon cider vinegar
1 tablespoon maple syrup
1 tablespoon olive oil
4 leaves fresh basil, finely chopped
4 plum tomatoes, chopped
salt (to taste)
pepper (to taste)

Preheat oven to 230°C/450°F/gas mark 8. In a large bowl, combine the carrots, courgette, mushrooms, peppers, onions, and garlic. Drizzle with a touch of oil and mix well. Lay them out on a baking sheet or roasting tin and roast them in the oven for 15-20 minutes, stirring occasionally, until vegetables are browned. When done, place 50g/2oz of the roasted vegetables into a blender or food processor and blend with the water, tomato purée, vinegar, maple syrup, oil, basil, and tomatoes. Transfer this sauce and the remaining roasted vegetables to a medium saucepan and cook on medium-high heat for 10 minutes. Add salt and pepper to taste. Simmer on low heat.

**Pie Crust:**

150g/5oz coarse cornmeal
850ml/28fl oz water
1 tablespoon oil

salt (to taste)
pepper (to taste)

In a medium bowl, whisk together the cornmeal with 250ml/8fl oz cold water, then set aside. In a medium pan, bring the remaining water to a boil. Once boiling, add the cornmeal mixture to the water and turn the heat down to medium-low. Add the oil, salt, and pepper. Continuously stir the mixture for about 10-15 minutes, until the mixture sticks together and becomes very stiff. Pour into a lightly oiled pie dish or a casserole dish. Let set for 5-10 minutes. Pour veggie topping into pie crust. Cut into slices. **Makes 4-6 servings.**

# BURNIN' BUTT BURRITOS

A masterpiece – a tasty and nutritious wrap. Beans and rice make a complementary protein when combined. For variety, add your favourite vegetables to the saucepan.

1/2 small onion, chopped
2 cloves garlic, crushed
50g/2oz broccoli, chopped
4 mushrooms, chopped
1/2 medium red pepper, chopped
1-3 jalapeño chillies, seeded and minced

2 tablespoons olive oil
4 large tortilla shells
275g/10oz re-fried beans (pg. 93)
soy cheese (optional)
salsa (pg. 86)
200g/7oz cooked rice

Preheat oven to 180°C/350°F/gas mark 4. In a medium saucepan, sauté the onions, garlic, broccoli, mushrooms, peppers, and jalapeños in the oil on medium-high heat until onions become translucent. Set aside. Lay tortilla shells down and spread a thin layer of re-fried beans, cheese, salsa, rice, and the veggie mixture on each.

Roll up and lay on baking sheet. Bake burritos for 15-20 minutes. Serve topped with salsa or guacamole (pg. 85). **Makes 4 burritos.**

# ARTICHOKE PASTA

This unique pasta dish combines capers, artichoke hearts, and sun-dried tomatoes, giving it a tangy, sparkly flavour.

cooked pasta shapes (enough for 4 people)
1 small onion, chopped
450g jar marinated artichoke hearts, chopped (don't drain; use the oil to cook with)
4-6 cloves garlic, crushed
1 tablespoon lemon juice
4-6 sun-dried tomatoes, chopped

3 tablespoons capers, drained
1 teaspoon thyme
2 teaspoons dried basil
salt (to taste)
pepper (to taste)
faux Parmesan cheese (garnish) (pg.154)

While pasta is cooking, in a medium saucepan sauté the onions in 2 tablespoons of the artichoke oil on medium-high heat until the onions are translucent. Add the artichokes, garlic, and lemon juice. Cook for another 5 minutes, until the sauce has reduced. Scoop out 4 tablespoons of pasta water and add to the saucepan, along with the sun-dried tomatoes, capers, thyme, basil, salt, and pepper. Cook about 2 minutes, until tomatoes are warmed through. Drain pasta and toss with sauce. Garnish with Parmesan. **Makes 4 servings.**

# FRAGRANT GARLIC PARSLEY PASTA

Simplicity at its finest. A zesty and lively dish that, when teamed with garlic bread (pg. 79), is sure to knock your dinner partners' socks off.

cooked pasta (enough for 2 people)
8-12 cloves garlic, crushed
1 teaspoon red chilli flakes
1 teaspoon salt

1 tablespoon olive oil
2 tablespoons flax oil
40g/1½ oz fresh parsley, chopped
faux Parmesan cheese (optional) (pg. 154)

While pasta is cooking, in a small saucepan, sauté the garlic, chilli flakes, and salt in oil on medium-low heat until garlic is tender. Set aside. Drain pasta and toss with flax oil, parsley, and the garlic mixture. Garnish with Parmesan if desired and serve. **Makes 2 servings.**

# CREAMY CURRIED VEGGIES

Rich and full of flavour, this dish is at its best when served over rice.

1 large onion, sliced
2-6 cloves garlic, crushed
1-3 large carrots, diced
2 tablespoons olive oil
1 medium potato, cubed
175g/6oz cauliflower florets, sliced
6-8 mushrooms, sliced

1 tablespoon curry powder
½ teaspoon cumin
½ teaspoon turmeric
pinch of cayenne pepper
250ml/8fl oz coconut milk or soy milk
115g/4oz peas
3 tablespoons Braggs or soy sauce

In a large saucepan, sauté the onions, garlic, and carrots in oil on medium-high heat until the onions become translucent. Add the vegetables, curry, cumin, turmeric, and cayenne pepper, stirring often so they don't stick to the pan, cooking for 2-4 minutes. Add the milk, cover, and reduce the heat to medium-low. Simmer for 10-20 minutes, stirring occasionally, until potatoes can be pierced easily with a fork. Stir in the peas and Braggs, and cook uncovered on medium-high heat stirring constantly until the liquid has thickened. Serve over rice or noodles. Note: you can use whatever vegetables you have kicking around (e.g., spinach, kale, spring onions). **Makes 2-4 servings.**

# CLASSIC SPINACH LASAGNE

Mamma mia! A mouthwatering take on an Italian favourite. You can use matzo or tortilla chips in place of noodles if you want to be cheeky!

450g/1lb medium tofu
4 tablespoons soy milk
1 teaspoon dried oregano
3 teaspoons dried basil
1 teaspoon salt
2 tablespoons lemon juice
4 cloves garlic, crushed

1 small onion, chopped
115g/4oz spinach, chopped
1-1.5 litres/1³/4 -2¹/2 pints tomato sauce
  (pgs. 76-77)
cooked (or non-cook) lasagne sheets
225g/8oz soy cheese for topping (optional)

Preheat oven to 180°C/350°F/gas mark 4. In a blender or food processor, blend the tofu, milk, oregano, basil, salt, lemon juice, garlic, and onions together until it achieves the consistency of cottage cheese. If the mixture is too thick, add a little water. Stir in the chopped spinach and set aside.

Cover the bottom of a roasting tin with a thin layer of tomato sauce, then a layer of lasagne. Sprinkle half of the tofu mixture and 50g/2oz of the optional cheese. Cover this with lasagne and a layer of sauce. Add the remaining filling, 50g/2oz of cheese, and a layer of sauce. Add one more layer of lasagne, and cover with sauce. Top with remaining cheese. Bake for 30-45 minutes. Remove from oven and let sit 10 minutes before serving. **Makes 4-6 servings.**

# MUM'S BEAN & CHEESE CASSEROLE

This was my favourite recipe that my mum used to make for my brother and me. **S**

5-6 small potatoes, sliced
1 tablespoon mustard
300g/11oz cooked or canned baked beans (pg.93)

1-2 teaspoons pepper
115-225g/4-8oz soy cheese

Preheat oven to 200°C/400°F/gas mark 6. In a large pan of water, boil the sliced potatoes until they can be pierced easily with a fork. Meanwhile, in a small bowl, stir together the mustard, beans, and pepper, and set aside. Drain the potatoes and place half of them onto a lightly oiled casserole dish. Add half of the bean mixture on top, then half of cheese. Repeat. Cover and bake for 35-40 minutes. **Makes 2-4 servings.**

# PARMESAN CRUSTED VEGGIE SANDWICHES

Hot and crispy on the outside, cool and fresh on the inside. This secret sandwich recipe will ensure that you never need to visit the corner deli again.

4 tablespoons margarine
25g/1oz soy Parmesan cheese
salt (to taste)
pepper (to taste)
8 thick slices firm bread
1³/4 tablespoons soy mayonnaise (pg. 151)

1¹/2 tablespoons Dijon mustard
2 avocados, sliced
1 medium tomato, sliced thinly into 12 slices
1 small red onion, sliced
175g/6oz alfalfa sprouts

In a food processor or small bowl, blend together the margarine, Parmesan, salt, and pepper. Spread a portion of the margarine mixture on one side of each slice of bread. Fry bread slices in batches on a non-stick frying pan on medium-high heat for about 3 minutes, until crisp and deep brown. When done, set toast aside to cool.

In a small bowl, blend the mayonnaise and mustard together. On a piece of toast, spread a layer of the mayo mixture, avocado, tomatoes, onions, and sprouts. Place another toast slice on top. **Makes 4 sandwiches.**

# KIERAN'S FAVOURITE RICE

Our friends Jen and Chris have the most beautiful little girl named Kieran. This is her favourite rice dish. Once you try it, it will be your favourite, too.

1 large onion, chopped

2-8 cloves garlic, chopped

1/2 teaspoon salt

2 tablespoons olive oil

550ml/18fl oz tomato juice

450g/1lb firm tofu, cubed

1 medium green pepper, chopped

1 stalk broccoli, chopped

2 medium carrots, chopped

3-6 mushrooms, chopped

(plus whatever other vegetables you may have)

400g/14oz cooked or canned kidney beans

1/2 teaspoon dried basil

1/2 teaspoon dried oregano

pepper (to taste)

cayenne pepper (to taste)

350g/12oz white basmati rice

120-250ml/5-8fl oz water (only if you don't have enough liquid to cook the rice)

2 medium tomatoes, chopped

50g/2oz green or black olives (optional)

In a large saucepan, sauté the onions, garlic, and salt in the oil on medium-high heat until the onions become translucent. Add the tomato juice, tofu, peppers, broccoli, carrots, mushrooms, and beans. Stir gently, so as not to make the tofu mushy. Add the basil, oregano, pepper, cayenne pepper, and rice. Again, stir gently. If you think there isn't enough liquid to cook the rice, then add a little water.

Cover with a lid, bring to a boil, then reduce heat and let simmer 15-25 minutes or until rice is done. Add the fresh tomatoes and olives. Stir and cover. Let simmer until most of the liquid has been absorbed. Remove from heat, fluff with fork before serving. **Makes 4-6 servings.**

# SAVOURY SHEPHERD'S PIE

This delightful dish is sure to have guests coming back for seconds. It tastes best when topped with miso gravy (pg. 75).

**Filling:**
1 small or medium onion, chopped
3 small carrots, chopped
25g/1oz spinach, chopped
1 stalk celery, chopped
1 large tomato, chopped
2 tablespoons olive oil
115g/4oz cooked or canned green lentils, mashed
1/2 teaspoon dried basil

1/2 teaspoon salt
1 tablespoon Braggs or soy sauce

**Topping:**
3 medium potatoes, cooked and roughly chopped
4 tablespoons soy milk
1 tablespoon margarine or olive oil
salt to taste

Preheat oven to 180°C/350°F/gas mark 4. In a medium pan of water, boil the chopped potatoes until they can be pierced easily with a fork. In a medium saucepan, sauté the onions, carrots, spinach, celery, and tomatoes in the oil. Once carrots are tender, add the mashed lentils, basil, salt, and Braggs. Stir and simmer without a lid until the liquid cooks off.

Meanwhile, in a medium bowl, mash the potatoes, milk, margarine, and salt with a potato masher or fork. Set aside. Pour the vegetable mixture into a lightly oiled pie dish and then layer the mashed potatoes over the top. Bake for 15-20 minutes. **Makes 4-6 servings.**

# BIG BEN'S LENTIL BURGERS

My mum used to make this recipe. We called them Big Ben's burgers because my younger brother Ben was a miniature human garbage disposal with a big appetite. This was his favourite meal as a kid. **S**

130g/4½ oz wheatgerm
450g/1lb cooked or canned lentils
115g/4oz breadcrumbs
1/2 onion, chopped

3 tablespoons olive oil
1/2 teaspoon salt
1/2 teaspoon pepper

On a small plate, set aside 2 tablespoons of the wheatgerm for coating. In a medium bowl, stir together the remaining wheatgerm, lentils, breadcrumbs, onions, oil, salt, and pepper. Divide and shape into 4 patties. Lay down each patty in the wheatgerm, coating each side.

Cook in a lightly oiled frying pan on medium-high heat for 5-10 minutes, flipping occasionally. Serve like a regular burger – an all-vegan patty, special sauce, lettuce, soy cheese, pickles, onions on a sesame bun! **Makes 4 patties.**

# SPICY BLACK BEAN BURGERS

These burgers are spiced to perfection. To make them even spicier, you could melt jalapeño soy cheese on each patty and serve topped with salsa (pg. 86).

50g/2oz plain flour
1 small onion, diced
2 cloves garlic, crushed
1/2 teaspoon dried oregano
1 small hot or jalapeño chilli, finely chopped
1 tablespoon olive oil
1/2 medium red pepper, diced
300g/11oz cooked or canned black beans, mashed

75g/3oz sweetcorn kernels
50g/2oz breadcrumbs
1/4 teaspoon cumin
1/2 teaspoon salt
2 teaspoons chilli powder
2 tablespoons fresh parsley, finely chopped
   (optional)

On a small plate, set aside flour for coating. In a medium saucepan, sauté the onion, garlic, oregano, and hot chilli in oil on medium-high heat until the onions are translucent. Add the peppers and sauté another 2 minutes, until pepper is tender. Set aside. In a large bowl, mash the black beans with a potato masher or fork. Stir in the vegetables (including the sweetcorn), breadcrumbs, cumin, salt, chilli powder, and parsley. Mix well. Divide and shape into 5 or 6 patties. Lay down each patty in flour, coating each side. Cook in a lightly oiled frying pan on medium-high heat for 5-10 minutes or until browned on both sides. **Makes 4-6 patties.**

# VEGGIE RICE BURGERS

These make scrumptious and flavourful patties, but they're fragile, so treat them with tender loving care. Serve on a bun or bread with soy cheese, ketchup, and relish.

50g/2oz plain flour
1 medium carrot, diced
1 small onion, diced
40g/1 1/2 oz courgette, diced
1 stalk celery, chopped
2-4 mushrooms, chopped
2 cloves garlic, crushed
1/4 teaspoon thyme

1/4 teaspoon dried dill
1 tablespoon olive oil
200g/7oz cooked rice, mashed
1/4 teaspoon salt
1 tablespoon Braggs or soy sauce
1 tablespoon tahini
1 tablespoon psyllium husks

On a small plate, set aside flour for coating. In a medium saucepan, sauté the carrots, onions, courgette, celery, mushrooms, garlic, thyme, and dill in the oil until vegetables are tender. Remove from heat. In a large bowl, stir together the sautéed vegetables and cooked rice. Add the salt, Braggs, tahini, and psyllium husks. Mix together well. Divide and shape into 6 patties. Lay down each patty in flour, coating each side. Cook in a lightly oiled frying pan on medium-high heat for 5-10 minutes or until browned on both sides. **Makes 6 patties.**

# VEGAN SLOPPY JOES

A truly exceptional vegan dish. Bet you never thought you'd be able to have it again!

**Tomato Sauce:**
4 tablespoons olive oil
1 small onion, chopped
4 cloves garlic, crushed
175g/6oz tomato purée
2 medium or large tomatoes, chopped
1 teaspoon salt
1 teaspoon dried basil
1 teaspoon dried oregano
1 teaspoon pepper

250ml/8fl oz boiling water
250g/9oz textured vegetable protein (TVP)
1 medium onion, chopped
1 tablespoon oil
1 medium green pepper, chopped
1 medium tomato, chopped
1 large gherkin, chopped
2 tablespoons Braggs or soy sauce
1½ teaspoons chilli powder
dash each of cayenne pepper, allspice and salt

In a blender or food processor, blend together the oil, onion, garlic, tomato purée, tomatoes, salt, basil, oregano, and pepper until you reach the desired consistency. Set aside.

In a medium bowl, pour the boiling water over TVP and set aside for 10-15 minutes. In a medium saucepan, sauté the onions in oil on medium-high heat until translucent. Lower heat to medium and add the peppers, tomatoes, gherkin, Braggs, chilli powder, cayenne pepper, allspice, salt, and tomato sauce. Simmer for 5 minutes. Add TVP to saucepan and stir together. Simmer on medium-low heat for another 20-30 minutes and serve over toast or on a bun. **Makes 2-4 servings.**

# COURGETTE DELIGHT

Hard to believe that anything so easy to make could be so delicious.

175g/6oz soy mozzarella cheese, grated
2 x 400g cans chopped tomatoes
600g/1lb 6oz courgettes, chopped
½ teaspoon dried oregano
½ teaspoon dried basil

½ teaspoon red chilli flakes
½ teaspoon salt
225g/8oz cooked or canned lentils
115g/4oz jasmine rice

Preheat oven to 180°C/350°F/gas mark 4. In a large casserole dish, combine 50g/2oz of the cheese with the tomatoes, courgette, oregano, basil, red chilli flakes, salt, lentils, and the rice. Stir together. Top with remaining cheese and bake uncovered for 30-40 minutes or until rice is done. **Makes 2-4 servings.**

# POTATO "CHEESE" PEROGIES

These tasty jewels will explode in your mouth. Serve these up with a green salad or steamed veggies.

**Filling:**
2 medium or large potatoes, cubed
175g/6oz soy cheese, grated
1 tablespoon lemon juice
1 teaspoon Dijon mustard
1 teaspoon dried dill
dash of pepper

**Dough:**
175g/6oz plain flour
1/2 teaspoon salt
1/8 teaspoon nutmeg
egg replacer (to equal 2 eggs)
4 tablespoons margarine or vegetable shortening
sour cream (garnish) (pg. 152)
salsa (garnish) (pg. 86)

In a medium pan of water, boil the cubed potatoes until they can be pierced easily with a fork. Drain. In a medium bowl, combine the potatoes, cheese, lemon juice, mustard, dill, and pepper. Mash together well with a potato masher or fork. Set aside.

In a medium bowl, combine the flour, salt, nutmeg, and egg replacer. With your hands or a fork cut the margarine into the flour mixture until well blended. You will want a nice, smooth dough, so you may need to add a touch of water if the dough is dry. Divide the dough evenly into 16 balls. Roll out each ball into a 7.5cm/3in circle and put 1½ tablespoons of potato mixture in each centre. Fold dough over and press edges down with a fork.

In a large pan of boiling water, add 3-4 perogies at a time and cook for 5 minutes on low boil. Remove perogies with slotted spoon and serve. As an option, you could fry the perogies in a non-stick frying pan until crispy. Top the perogies with sour cream or salsa. **Makes 16 perogies.**

# JANA'S HEALTHY RICE

Try this with honey lemon carrots (pg. 87).

1 litre/1¾ pints water
400g/14oz short-grain brown rice
5 cloves garlic, crushed
3 tablespoons coriander, finely chopped
1/4 small white onion, chopped

1 tablespoon cider vinegar
3 tablespoons curry paste
1 teaspoon salt
4 tablespoons flax oil
225g/8oz kale, chopped

In a medium pan, add the water and rice, boil for 30 minutes on medium heat. Stir in the garlic, coriander, and onion and cook 10 minutes more. Remove from heat and stir in the vinegar, curry paste, salt, oil, and kale. **Makes 2-4 servings.**

# STUFFED SPAGHETTI SQUASH

Warm and homey, this is a perfect harvest-time concoction.

1 medium or large spaghetti squash
1 medium onion, chopped
4-6 mushrooms, chopped
1 tablespoon olive oil
1 teaspoon salt

1 teaspoon pepper
1/2 teaspoon cumin
225g/8oz cooked or canned lentils
50g/2oz breadcrumbs

Preheat oven to 180°C/350°F/gas mark 4. Cut the squash lengthwise in half and scoop out the seeds, but leave the meat. Lay squash face up on baking sheet. Set aside. In a medium saucepan, sauté the onions and mushrooms in oil on medium-high heat until onions are translucent. Add the salt, pepper, cumin, lentils, and breadcrumbs and cook for 3 minutes more. Spoon the stuffing into each half of squash and bake in oven for 30 minutes or until squash can be pierced easily with a fork. Note: If your squash won't lay flat on your baking sheet, you can cut a bit off the bottom.
**Makes 2-4 servings.**


# PIZZA

Pizza doesn't have to be about 4 different kinds of cheese or meat. In fact, your pizza doesn't even need cheese or meat at all! The combination possibilities are endless. Here are some of our favourites:

• tomato sauce, mushrooms, olives, spinach, soy cheese
• tomato sauce, artichoke hearts, garlic cloves, soy cheese
• tomato pesto sauce (pg. 76), red onion, pine nuts, soy cheese
• tomato sauce, sun dried tomatoes, fresh herbs, soy cheese
• pesto sauce (pg. 76), red, yellow and green peppers, garlic, fresh herbs
• tomato sauce, red onions, black olives, capers, marjoram

# YEAST PIZZA CRUST

400ml/14fl oz tepid water
10g/1/4oz packet yeast
1 teaspoon salt
350g/12oz plain flour

Preheat oven to 180°C/350°F/gas mark 4. In a medium ceramic bowl, whisk together the water and yeast until dissolved. Add the salt and whisk again. Stir in the flour and knead dough for about 3 minutes. Set aside and let dough rise for 20 minutes in a warm, draught-free place. Knead again and if dough is too sticky, add a bit more flour. Let dough rise for another 10-20 minutes. Roll out dough onto a pizza pan and prick dough all over with a fork before adding all your goodies. Bake for 30-40 minutes.

# YEAST-FREE PIZZA CRUST

225g/8oz plain flour
50g/2oz soy Parmesan cheese
1/2 teaspoon salt
1 tablespoon dried oregano
1 tablespoon dried basil
4 tablespoons margarine
5 tablespoons olive oil
5 tablespoons cold water

Preheat oven to 200°C/400°F/gas mark 6. In a food processor or with your hands, mix the flour, Parmesan, salt, oregano, basil, margarine, and oil until "just mixed". Spoon the flour mixture into a medium or large bowl and slowly add the water while you knead the dough. Knead only for a few minutes until dough is pliable. Form into a 15cm/6in disc and let chill in refrigerator for 20 minutes. Roll out dough onto a pizza pan and prick all over with a fork before adding all your goodies. Bake for 20 minutes.

# MATZO PIZZA

4 matzos
250ml/8fl oz tomato sauce (pgs. 76-77)
toppings (e.g., mushrooms, spinach)
seasoning (e.g., garlic, oregano, basil)
soy cheese

Preheat oven to 180°C/350°F/gas mark 4. Lay matzos on baking sheet. Add 4 tablespoons sauce on each matzo. Add toppings, seasonings, and cheese. Bake 10-12 minutes or until cheese has melted.

# TOFURKY (TOFU TURKEY)

For your vegan festivities. Serve topped with gravy (pg. 75), mashed potatoes (pg. 88), cranberry sauce (pg. 79), and assorted steamed veggies.

**Marinade:**
350ml/12fl oz boiling water
1/2 tablespoon dill
1/2 teaspoon rosemary
1/2 teaspoon thyme
1/2 teaspoon marjoram

1/2 teaspoon sage
1/2 teaspoon pepper
1-4 cloves garlic, thinly sliced
3 tablespoons olive oil
450g/1lb firm tofu, 5mm/1/4 in thick

In a large bowl, whisk together the water, dill, rosemary, thyme, marjoram, salt, pepper, garlic, and oil. Set aside. Slice the tofu into desired shapes, about 5mm/1/4 in thick. (I usually cut the tofu into 10 x 5mm/1/4 in squares.)

Lay each slice down on a baking sheet or a roasting tin, cover with marinade, and let sit for 1 hour or more (the longer the better). Preheat oven to 180°C/350°F/gas mark 4. Bake for 60 minutes, turning slices over after 30 minutes.

To serve, fry tofurky cutlets in a non-stick frying pan until both sides are browned.
**Makes 10 slices.**

# "ANYTHING GOES" VEGETABLE STIR-FRY

Using seasonal vegetables will change the character of this fast and easy stir-fry. Remember to begin with the denser vegetables first (carrots, squash, etc.) and the more delicate vegetables later (pak choi, kale, peas, etc.).

2 medium carrots, chopped
1 head of broccoli, chopped (including stems)
4-6 mushrooms, chopped
450g/1lb medium or firm tofu, cubed
splash of olive oil
2 stalks celery, chopped

2-4 leaves pak choi, roughly chopped
2 handfuls vegetables of your choice (e.g., sugar
  snap peas, kale, bean sprouts)
Braggs (garnish)
flax oil (garnish)
gomashio (garnish) (pg. 154)

In a large wok or frying pan, sauté the carrots, broccoli stems, mushrooms, and tofu in oil on medium-high heat until carrots are tender. Add the broccoli florets, celery, pak choi, and vegetables of your choice and simmer on medium-high heat until al dente. Serve over rice, noodles, or on its own and garnish with Braggs, flax oil, and gomashio. **Makes 2-4 servings.**

# CORRI'S GAGGLE OF GREEN GOO

My friend Corri is just learning the joys of cooking. This is her latest creation.
Try serving it over rice or noodles. **S**

115g/4oz firm tofu, cubed
1/2 medium green pepper, chopped
1-2 stalks celery, chopped
40g/1 1/2 oz mushrooms, chopped

1 tablespoon olive oil
1-2 tablespoons coriander chutney (or other green chutney)
350g/12oz pak choi, chopped

In a large saucepan or wok, sauté the tofu, peppers, celery, and mushrooms in oil on medium-high heat until the celery turns tender. Stir in the chutney, then add the pak choi (but don't stir it in), cover with a lid, and cook on medium heat for 10-15 minutes. Stir once and then cook for another five minutes without a lid to blend the flavours. **Makes 2 servings.**

# CORRI'S EASY GREEN CHOP SUEY

Corri thinks her recipe tastes like good chop suey. Try it and see. Serve over rice or noodles, and garnish with gomashio (pg. 154).

115g/4oz firm tofu, cubed
2 stalks celery, chopped
4-8 mushrooms, chopped
1 tablespoon olive oil
350g/12oz pak choi, chopped
2 tablespoons miso

2 tablespoons water
1 teaspoon fresh ginger, finely grated
2 tablespoons Braggs
3 spring onions, chopped
115g/4oz fresh spinach, roughly chopped
dash of salt

In a large saucepan or wok, sauté the tofu, celery, and mushrooms in oil on medium-high heat until tofu starts to turn golden. Add the pak choi (but don't stir it in), cover with a lid, and cook over medium heat for 10 minutes. In a small bowl, whisk together the miso, water, ginger, and Braggs. Pour over the vegetables and stir together. Add the onions and spinach, but again don't stir them in. Add salt and cover for another 5 minutes. Stir it all together before serving. **Makes 2 servings.**

# VEGAN BREADS
# & MUFFINS

We don't like to use baking yeast in our bread or biscuit recipes. To make our loaves light and fluffy, we regularly use sour dough starter, baking powder, bicarbonate of soda, and vinegar. With a delicate combination of these ingredients, we are able to produce results that we are most happy with. We believe unyeasted bread is a more holistic and traditional approach to eating. In terms of health benefits, unyeasted bread is easier for the body to digest and also helps to keep disorders like candida away.  An important thing to remember too when baking vegan is that you are not using any of the usual things that help to bind your ingredients and make your baked goods fluffy and light.

It's best if you're able to find/buy/borrow a "bread only" bowl. Try to find a beautiful ceramic or wooden bowl, as they make the best bread palette. A word of caution: never use metal bowls for making bread, as they may deactivate the rising ability of the bread mixture.  Here are some tips to make your baking work:

## Sift

Using a sieve to mix all your dry ingredients together helps to keep things light. Always mix your dry ingredients together before you add any wet!

## Don't overmix

When mixing, use a wooden spoon or your hands to gently mix the dry and wet ingredients together. You want to mix "just" enough to blend all the ingredients together. But avoid mixing too vigorously, as your baking will end up flat and heavy.

## Keep it moist

A  small pan of  water in the oven  while baking  will help to keep your baking moist.

## Don't expect shop-bought goodies

Remember that you're baking vegan now, so your breads and muffins  won't look exactly like those from the local bakery. But don't forget, taste is everything! So before you dismiss your creations, take a bite!

## Check for readiness

Poke your breads and muffins with a clean knife or fork before taking them out of the oven. If it comes out clean, it's ready; if it's still gooey, wait another 5 minutes, then test again.

# OATMEAL BREAD

Due to the wonderful nature of oat flour, this bread is deliciously moist and sweet. This recipe is perfect for anyone who wants an almost gluten-free bread. Note: You can make this bread wheat-free by using kamut or other wheat-free flours.

350g/12oz plain flour
115g/4oz oatmeal flour
   (to make oatmeal flour, put 150g/5oz of oatmeal
   in food processor and blend well)
2 teaspoons baking powder
1 teaspoon bicarbonate of soda

1 teaspoon salt
2 tablespoons sweetener
egg replacer (to equal 1 egg)
475ml/16fl oz  soy milk
1 teaspoon vinegar

Preheat oven to 190°C/375°F/gas mark 5. In a large bowl, sift together the flours, baking powder, bicarbonate of soda, salt, and sweetener. In a separate smaller bowl, whisk together the egg replacer with the milk and vinegar and add to the flour mixture. Mix together carefully until "just mixed". Place in a lightly oiled 450g/1lb loaf tin or shape into an oval loaf and place on a lightly oiled baking sheet.

Dust top of loaf with oatmeal flakes and bake for 35–45 minutes. Test with a knife to see if done.
**Makes 1 loaf.**

# SODA BREAD

This stout, dense loaf is a knockout.

225g/8oz plain flour
225g/8oz pastry flour
2 tablespoons arrowroot powder or cornflour
2 teaspoons baking powder
1½ teaspoons bicarbonate of soda
1 teaspoon salt

2 tablespoons egg replacer
350ml/12fl oz water
3–4 tablespoons sweetener
3–4 tablespoons oil
2 tablespoons vinegar
25g/1oz ground almonds (optional)

Preheat oven to 190°C/375°F/gas mark 5. In a large bowl, sift together the flours, arrowroot powder, baking powder, bicarbonate of soda, and salt. Add the egg replacer, water, sweetener, oil, vinegar, and optional nuts, and mix together until "just mixed". Spoon into a lightly oiled 450g/1lb loaf tin and brush the top with oil. Bake for 55–60 minutes. Test with a knife to see if done.
**Makes 1 loaf.**

# THE ART OF SOURDOUGH BREAD

There is a definite art to making sourdough bread; it requires patience and time. So if your loaves don't turn out the way you feel they should, don't get discouraged, just try again. Here are a few tips if your loaves aren't turning out they way you want them to:

**Not rising enough:** add a bit more starter
**Too gooey:** add a bit more flour
**Too lumpy:** knead the bread a little longer
**Cracks:** cut some slits in the top of the loaf right before baking

# SOURDOUGH STARTER

250ml/8fl oz water

115g/4oz wholemeal flour

In a large, clean, dry jar, stir together the water and flour until completely mixed. Cover jar with a cotton cloth and leave for 3-5 days in a warm, draught-free spot (the top of the refrigerator is a good spot). Stir every 12 hours. On the third day, it's ready. The starter should be bubbly and smell sour. If it smells rancid, throw it out and start again. Store in the fridge with a tight-fitting lid.

As you use your starter for baking, you can keep the rest of it indefinitely by "feeding" it. If you use 125ml/4fl oz of starter, for instance, refill it by adding 50g/2oz flour and 125ml/4fl oz water to the balance. Stir and let sit for 3 hours before returning to storage. If you don't use your starter often, it will become dormant. To revive it, add 15g/1/2 oz flour and 2 tablespoons of warm water, and keep it in a warm place for 10-12 hours before using.

# SOURDOUGH BREAD

500-800g/11/4 -13/4 lb wholemeal pastry flour*
600ml/1 pint water

120-175ml/4-6fl oz sourdough starter
1 teaspoon salt

*You can vary your flour for different tastes and textures: e.g., 450g/1lb pastry, 350g/12oz spelt.
In a large bowl, stir together 500g/11/4 lb of flour, water, starter, and salt. Slowly add the remaining flour, 50g/2oz at a time, while gently kneading the dough until smooth and consistent. Place dough in a lightly oiled ceramic bowl. Roll the dough around so that it's covered in oil. Cover the bowl with a cotton cloth and let dough rise for 12 hours.

Re-knead dough for 3-5 minutes. Cut it in half and either place in loaf tins or shape into 2 loaves and place on baking sheet. Cover and let dough rise 6 more hours, until the dough doubles in size.

Preheat oven to 220°C/425°F/gas mark 7. Bake loaves for 15 minutes, then reduce heat to 180°C/350°F/gas mark 4 and bake for another 45 minutes or until golden brown. Check with knife to see if done. **Makes 2 loaves.**

# EASY BISCUITS

These tasty jewels are perfect smothered in miso gravy (pg. 75) or simply teamed with any soup.

225g/8oz plain flour
3 teaspoons baking powder
1 teaspoon salt

50g/2oz margarine or vegetable shortening
175-250ml/6-8fl oz sour soy milk (soy milk plus 1 teaspoon vinegar)

Preheat oven to 230°C/450°F/gas mark 8. In a large bowl, sift together the flour, baking powder, and salt. Add the margarine and sour milk and mix together gently until "just mixed". Spoon into lightly oiled muffin tins, or roll out and cut with biscuit cutters and place on a lightly oiled baking sheet. Bake for 12-18 minutes. **Makes 6 biscuits.**

# SOURDOUGH BISCUITS

Enjoy the delicious flavour of sourdough in a biscuit. They stand well on their own or served with a meal.

225g/8oz plain flour
1/2 teaspoon salt
2 teaspoons bicarbonate of soda

1 tablespoon sweetener
115g/4oz margarine
350ml/12fl oz sourdough starter (pg. 115)

Preheat oven to 220°C/425°F/gas mark 7. In a large bowl, sift together the flour, salt, bicarbonate of soda, and sweetener. Cut in the margarine and mix well. Stir in the sourdough starter. Knead lightly until "just mixed". Spoon into lightly oiled muffin tins, or roll out and cut with biscuit cutters and place on lightly oiled baking sheet. Bake for 10-12 minutes. **Makes 6-12 biscuits.**

# FANCY BISCUITS

These scrumptious scrumpets boast a savoury flavour all their own.

225g/8oz plain flour
2 teaspoons baking powder
1/2 teaspoon salt
2 tablespoons vegetable oil or shortening

250ml/8fl oz sour soy milk (soy milk plus 1 teaspoon vinegar)
40g/1 1/2 oz spring onions, chopped
1 tablespoon dried dill
1/4 teaspoon pepper

Preheat oven to 230°C/450°F/gas mark 8. In a large bowl, sift together the flour, baking powder, and salt. Add the oil, sour milk, onions, dill, and pepper and mix together gently until "just mixed". Spoon into lightly oiled muffin tins. Bake for 12-18 minutes. **Makes 6 biscuits.**

# SWEET BISCUITS

Try serving these biscuits with tea.

275g/10oz plain flour
25g/1oz dry sweetener
2 teaspoons baking powder

175g/6oz margarine
250ml/8fl oz soy milk

Preheat oven to 200°C/400°F/gas mark 6. In a large bowl, sift together the flour, sweetener, and baking powder. Stir in the margarine and milk and mix together until "just mixed". Spoon into lightly oiled muffin tins, or roll out and cut with biscuit cutters and place on lightly oiled baking sheet. Bake for 12-18 minutes. **Makes 8 biscuits.**

# CHAPATIS

This flat bread has it origins in India and goes great with curries or exquisite rice salad (pg.64).

175g/6oz plain flour
1/2 teaspoon salt

2 tablespoons oil
175-250ml/6-8fl oz water

In a large ceramic bowl, stir together the flour, salt, and oil. Slowly add the water to form a soft dough. Knead for 5 minutes. Cover bowl and dough with a tea towel and let stand for 30-60 minutes. Divide dough into 14 equal pieces and shape into balls. With a rolling pin, roll each ball into a 15cm/6in disc and fry in a dry frying pan over medium heat. Cook each side until browned, and serve warm. **Makes 14 chapatis.**

# FLAX SEED CRACKERS

The flax seed is a nutritious, versatile seed with many proven beneficial properties. For variation, add 1 teaspoon of oregano, onion powder, or dill. You can use hemp seeds instead of flax for this recipe.

65g/2½ oz flax seeds
175g/6oz plain flour
½ teaspoon baking powder
½ teaspoon salt
4 teaspoons margarine or vegetable shortening

1 tablespoon dried oregano (optional) or
   onion powder (optional) or
   dried dill (optional)
125ml/4fl oz soy milk

Preheat oven to 160°C/325°F/gas mark 3. In a food processor or with your hands, blend together the flax seeds, flour, baking powder, salt, margarine, and optional spices until well mixed. Place in a medium bowl and slowly add the milk. Mix and knead together until the dough forms a ball. Chill dough for 10-20 minutes.

Divide dough into 4 equal parts. In between 2 sheets of greaseproof paper, roll out the dough very thinly to form a rectangle. Cut into 6 squares, or use biscuit cutters. Repeat with remaining dough. Transfer crackers onto a lightly oiled baking sheet and bake for 15 minutes, then flip them over and bake for 5 minutes more. **Makes 24 crackers.**

# HARVEST HERB BREAD

The classic combination of these herbs bring flavour and life to this delicious bread.

175g/6oz plain flour
½ teaspoon salt
1½ teaspoons baking powder
½ teaspoon bicarbonate of soda
¼ teaspoon dried marjoram
⅛ teaspoon dried oregano
½ teaspoon dried basil
pinch of dried thyme

65g/2½ oz raisins
50g/2oz chopped nuts (optional)
egg replacer (to equal 1 egg)
2 tablespoons sweetener
4 tablespoons oil
1 teaspoon vinegar
175ml/6fl oz soy milk

Preheat oven to 200°C/400°F/gas mark 6. In a large bowl, sift together the flour, salt, baking powder, and bicarbonate of soda. Add the marjoram, oregano, basil, thyme, raisins, nuts, egg replacer, sweetener, oil, vinegar, and milk. Mix together gently until "just mixed". Spoon into a lightly oiled loaf tin and bake for 20-30 minutes. Test with a knife to see if done. **Makes 1 loaf.**

# SWEET POTATO CORN BREAD

A sweet, savoury bread to accompany soups.

115g/4oz plain flour
1 teaspoon baking powder
1/2 teaspoon bicarbonate of soda
1/2 teaspoon salt
1/8 teaspoon allspice
50g/2oz cornmeal
300g/11oz sweet potatoes, cooked and mashed

4 tablespoons oil
4 tablespoons sweetener
egg replacer (to equal 2 eggs)
125ml/4fl oz sour soy milk (soy milk plus
    1/2 tablespoon vinegar)

Preheat oven to 190°C/375°F/gas mark 5. In a large bowl, sift together the flour, baking powder, bicarbonate of soda, salt, and allspice. Stir in the cornmeal. Add the mashed sweet potatoes, oil, sweetener, egg replacer, and sour milk. Mix together gently until "just mixed". Spoon into a lightly oiled square or round loaf tin and bake for 30 minutes. Test with a knife to see if done. **Makes 1 loaf.**

# CINNAMON RAISIN BREAD

What could be a more fantastic aroma to wake up to than fresh cinnamon raisin bread hot out of the toaster?

115g/4oz plain flour
115g/4oz rye flour
1/2 teaspoon salt
1 1/2 teaspoons baking powder
1 teaspoon bicarbonate of soda
1/2 teaspoon allspice
1/4 teaspoon nutmeg

2 teaspoons cinnamon
250ml/8fl oz sour soy milk
    (soy milk plus 1 tablespoon vinegar)
50g/2oz sweetener
65g/2 1/2 oz raisins
50g/2oz chopped nuts

Preheat oven to 180°C/350°F/gas mark 4. In a large bowl, sift together the flours, salt, baking powder, bicarbonate of soda, allspice, nutmeg and cinnamon. Stir in the sour milk, sweetener, raisins, and nuts. Mix together gently until "just mixed". Spoon into a lightly oiled 450g/1lb loaf tin and bake for 45-50 minutes. Test with a knife to see if done. Let the bread sit for 10 minutes before slicing. **Makes 1 loaf.**

# APPLE SAUCE BREAD

Be tempted by this fruity-tasting bread. Serve toasted with nut butter and jam.

225g/8oz plain flour
2 teaspoons baking powder
1/2 teaspoon salt
1 teaspoon cinnamon
1/4 teaspoon nutmeg
40g/1 1/2 oz wheatgerm

egg replacer (to equal 2 eggs)
5 tablespoons maple syrup
5 tablespoons oil
350g/12oz apple sauce
75g/3oz nuts, chopped
1 teaspoon vinegar

Preheat oven to 180°C/350°F/gas mark 4. In a large bowl, stir together the flour, baking powder, salt, cinnamon, nutmeg, and wheatgerm. Add the egg replacer, maple syrup, oil, apple sauce, nuts, and vinegar. Mix together gently until "just mixed". Spoon the batter into a lightly oiled 450g/1lb loaf tin and bake for 50-55 minutes. Test with a knife to see if done. **Makes 1 loaf.**

# GINGER BREAD

Ginger is known for its healing properties and spicy taste. It turns this already dynamic loaf into a spicy treat.

350g/12oz plain flour
2 1/2 teaspoons baking powder
1/2 teaspoon bicarbonate of soda
1/2 teaspoon salt
1 teaspoon allspice
egg replacer (to equal 2 eggs)
125ml/4fl oz oil

125ml/4fl oz molasses
250ml/8fl oz soy milk
1 teaspoon vinegar
3-6 tablespoons fresh ginger, grated
75g/3oz crystallized ginger, chopped (optional)
50g/2oz walnuts

Preheat oven to 180°C/350°F/gas mark 4. In a large bowl, sift together the flour, baking powder, bicarbonate of soda, salt, and allspice. Add the egg replacer, oil, molasses, milk, vinegar, ginger, optional crystallized ginger, and nuts. Mix together gently until "just mixed". Spoon the batter into a lightly oiled 450g/1lb loaf tin and bake for 50 minutes. Test with a knife to see if done. Cool for 10 minutes before slicing and serving. **Makes 1 loaf.**

# COURGETTE BREAD

This sweet, summer squash loaf makes an equally good impression as a light, healthy snack or a sensible dessert.

175g/6oz plain flour
2 teaspoons baking powder
1/2 teaspoon salt
1 1/2 teaspoons cinnamon
egg replacer (to equal 1 egg)
90g/3 1/2 oz sweetener
5 tablespoons oil

1 teaspoon vinegar
1 teaspoon vanilla extract
250g/9oz courgette, grated
65g/2 1/2 oz raisins
50g/2oz nuts, chopped
4 tablespoons water (optional)

Preheat oven to 180°C/350°F/gas mark 4. In a large bowl, sift together the flour, baking powder, salt, and cinnamon. Add the egg replacer, sweetener, oil, vinegar, and vanilla, and mix. Stir in the courgette, raisins, and nuts and mix together gently until "just mixed". Add a little water if the dough seems too dry. Spoon batter into a lightly oiled 450g/1lb loaf tin and bake for 45-50 minutes. Test with a knife to see if done. Cool for 10 minutes before slicing and serving.
Makes 1 loaf.

# RHUBARB BREAD

This summer spectacular is a classic combination of both sweet and tart.

275g/10oz plain flour
2 teaspoons baking powder
1/2 teaspoon bicarbonate of soda
1/2 teaspoon salt
1 teaspoon ground ginger or
    1 tablespoon fresh ginger, grated

egg replacer (to equal 1 egg)
90g/3 1/2 oz sweetener
125ml/4fl oz oil
125ml/4fl oz orange or apple juice
175g/6oz rhubarb, finely chopped
75g/3oz nuts, chopped

Preheat oven to 180°C/350°F/gas mark 4. In a large bowl, sift together the flour, baking powder, bicarbonate of soda, salt, and ginger. Stir in the egg replacer, sweetener, oil, juice, rhubarb, and nuts. Mix together gently until "just mixed". Spoon into a lightly oiled 450g/1lb loaf tin and bake for 35-40 minutes. Test with a knife to see if done. Cool for 10 minutes before slicing and serving.
Makes 1 loaf.

# APRICOT BREAD

Closely related to the peach, the apricot offers a sweet yet subtle flavour to this loaf.

225g/8oz plain flour
2 teaspoons baking powder
1 teaspoon bicarbonate of soda
1 teaspoon salt
1/4 teaspoon ground ginger or
3/4 tablespoon fresh ginger, grated
225g/8oz dried apricots, chopped

egg replacer (to equal 1 egg)
75g/3oz sweetener
2 tablespoons oil
250ml/8fl oz apricot or orange juice
1 teaspoon vinegar
1 teaspoon vanilla extract
50g/2oz nuts, chopped

Preheat oven to 180°C/350°F/gas mark 4. In a large bowl, sift together the flour, baking powder, bicarbonate of soda, salt, and ginger. Stir in the apricots, egg replacer, sweetener, oil, juice, vinegar, vanilla, and nuts. Mix together gently until "just mixed". Spoon the batter into a lightly oiled 450g/1lb loaf tin and bake for 50 minutes. Test with a knife to see if done. Cool for 10 minutes before slicing and serving. **Makes 1 loaf.**

# BANANA BREAD

Simply the world's greatest loaf. For added sweetness, add 75g/3oz of chocolate chips to this recipe.

3 ripe bananas, mashed
1 tablespoon lemon juice
125ml/4fl oz oil
50g/2oz sweetener
130g/4 1/2 oz chopped dates

175g/6oz plain flour
75g/3oz wheatgerm
1/2 teaspoon salt
1/2 teaspoon baking powder
1/2 teaspoon bicarbonate of soda

Preheat oven to 190°C/375°F/gas mark 5. In a small bowl, mash the bananas with a fork until very mushy, then add the lemon juice, oil, sweetener, and dates and stir together. In a separate large bowl, stir together the flour, wheatgerm, salt, baking powder, and bicarbonate of soda. Add the banana mixture to the flour mixture and mix together gently until "just mixed". Spoon into a lightly oiled 450g/1lb loaf tin and bake for 40-50 minutes. Test with a knife to see if done. **Makes 1 loaf.**

# SPICY SOUP MUFFINS

Warm, spicy, and fragrant, these muffins are sure to please.

115g/4oz plain flour
115g/4oz rye flour
2 teaspoons baking powder
1/2 teaspoon bicarbonate of soda
1/2 teaspoon salt
1/2 teaspoon pepper
1/2 teaspoon nutmeg
3/4 teaspoon cinnamon
1/2 teaspoon fresh ginger, grated

1/4 teaspoon allspice
65g/21/2 oz raisins
egg replacer (to equal 2 eggs)
115g/4oz apple sauce
50g/2oz sweetener
150ml/1/4 pint sour soy milk (soy milk plus 1
    teaspoon vinegar)
4 tablespoons oil

Preheat oven to 200°C/400°F/gas mark 6. In a large bowl, stir together the flours, baking powder, bicarbonate of soda, salt, pepper, nutmeg, cinnamon, ginger, and allspice. Add the raisins, egg replacer, apple sauce, sweetener, sour milk, and oil. Mix together gently until "just mixed". Spoon the batter into lightly oiled muffin tins, filling them until about 2/3 full. Bake for 15-20 minutes. **Makes 6 muffins.**

# MAPLE-NUT SOUP MUFFINS

Try these delicious muffins as an accompaniment to any of our hearty soup recipes.

150g/5oz plain flour
11/2 teaspoons baking powder
1 teaspoon bicarbonate of soda
1/2 teaspoon salt
1/2 teaspoon cinnamon
4 tablespoons apple syrup

egg replacer (to equal 2 eggs)
150ml/1/4 pint sour soy milk (soy milk plus 3/4
    teaspoon vinegar)
4 tablespoons oil
75g/3oz pecans, chopped

Preheat oven to 200°C/400°F/gas mark 6. In a large bowl, sift together the flour, baking powder, bicarbonate of soda, salt, and cinnamon. Add the maple syrup, egg replacer, sour milk, oil, and pecans. Mix together gently until "just mixed". Spoon the batter into lightly oiled muffin tins, filling them until about 2/3 full. Bake for 15-20 minutes. **Makes 6 muffins.**

# COUNTRY CORN MUFFINS

Perfect alongside a piping hot bowl of quick and easy chilli (pg. 95).

75g/3oz yellow cornmeal
75g/3oz plain flour
1 teaspoon baking powder
1/2 teaspoon bicarbonate of soda
1/4 teaspoon salt
egg replacer (to equal 2 eggs)

50-125ml/2-4fl oz soy milk or water
2 tablespoons sweetener
2 tablespoons oil
1/2 teaspoon vinegar
175g/6oz sweetcorn kernels

Preheat oven to 180°C/350°F/gas mark 4. In a large bowl, stir together cornmeal, flour, baking powder, bicarbonate of soda, and salt. Add the egg replacer, milk, sweetener, oil, vinegar, and sweetcorn. Mix together gently until "just mixed". Spoon mixture into lightly oiled muffin tins, filling them to the top. Bake for 15 -20 minutes. Test with a knife to see if done. Cool for 5 minutes on a wire rack before serving. **Makes 6 muffins.**

# APPLE SAUCE MUFFINS

The aroma of these sweet scented muffins will arouse any tastebud and lead you into the kitchen.

225g/8oz plain flour
1/2 teaspoon salt
1 teaspoon bicarbonate of soda
1/2 teaspoon cinnamon
125ml/4fl oz soy milk

1 tablespoon cider vinegar
2 tablespoons oil
5 tablespoons maple syrup
225g/8oz apple sauce
200g/7oz raisins

Preheat oven to 190°C/375°F/gas mark 5. In a large bowl, sift together the flour, salt, bicarbonate of soda, and cinnamon. Add the milk, vinegar, oil, maple syrup, apple sauce, and raisins. Mix together gently until "just mixed". Spoon batter into lightly oiled muffin tins and bake for 15-20 minutes. Test with a knife to see if done. **Makes 6 muffins.**

# BLUE BANANA MUFFINS

A true masterpiece. After years of testing and development, we've perfected this muffin! Fearlessly indulge.

400g/14oz wholemeal pastry flour
2 teaspoons baking power
50g/2oz dry sweetener
125ml/4fl oz oil

350-475ml/12-16fl oz soy milk
2 bananas, mashed
2 tablespoons ground flax seed
115g/4oz blueberries

Preheat oven to 180°C/350°F/gas mark 4. In a large bowl, stir together the flour, baking powder, and sweetener. Add the oil, milk, mashed bananas, flax seeds, and blueberries. Mix together gently until "just mixed". Spoon into lightly oiled muffin tins and bake for 35-40 minutes. Test with a knife to see if done. **Makes 12 muffins.**

# RASPBERRY CORNMEAL MUFFINS

These are simply scrumptious. An ideal brunch item or mid-day pick-me-up.

175g/6oz cornmeal
175g/6oz plain flour
dash of salt
90g/3oz sweetener
3/4 teaspoon bicarbonate of soda

4 tablespoons oil
175ml/6fl oz soy milk
175ml/6fl oz orange or apple juice
1 teaspoon vinegar
115g/4oz raspberries

Preheat oven to 200°C/400°F/gas mark 6. In a large bowl, stir together the cornmeal, flour, salt, sweetener, and bicarbonate of soda. Add the oil, milk, juice, vinegar, and berries. Mix together gently until "just mixed". Spoon into lightly oiled muffin tins and bake for 35-45 minutes. Test with a knife to see if done. **Makes 6 muffins.**

# VEGAN DESSERTS

What could be more satisfying after any meal than a delectable dessert? Some people think that vegan desserts are lacklustre and tasteless; au contraire, they're zesty and full of taste. These desserts have been designed to be more nutritious than traditional treats without having to scrimp on flavour or presentation. Use premium ingredients in your baking and dessert-making and you can be guaranteed the tastiest and most gratifying desserts. C'mon, you're worth it!

# CHARMING CHOCOLATE CUPCAKES

Cupcakes are great. They're easy to make, portable, and take the formality out of cake. It doesn't matter whether you serve them out of a plastic container or off a silver platter – your guests will love them.

250ml/8fl oz molasses
250ml/8fl oz soy milk
350g/12oz chocolate or carob chips
6 tablespoons oil
1 teaspoon vanilla extract

4 tablespoons cornflour
225g/8oz plain flour
1 teaspoon bicarbonate of soda
6 paper cake cases

Preheat oven to 190°C/375°F/gas mark 5. In a small saucepan, whisk together the molasses, half the milk, and the chips.

Cook on medium heat until chips have melted, stirring constantly with a spoon. Add the oil, vanilla, cornflour and stir until well mixed. Remove from heat and set aside. In a medium bowl, sift the flour and bicarbonate of soda together. Add the remaining milk and the chocolate mixture and stir. Spoon into paper cake cases and bake for 15-20 minutes. Test with a knife to see if done. Once cooled, you can top with icing (pg. 143). **Makes 6 cupcakes.**

# MAPLE WALNUT BROWNIES

165g/5¹/₂ oz plain flour
40g/1¹/₂ oz cocoa or carob powder
1¹/₂ teaspoons baking powder
¹/₂ teaspoon salt
175ml/6fl oz maple syrup

4 tablespoons apple juice or water
5 tablespoons oil
2 teaspoons vanilla extract
50g/2oz walnuts, chopped (optional)

Preheat oven to 180°C/350°F/gas mark 4. In a large bowl, sift together the flour, cocoa powder, baking powder, and salt. Add the maple syrup, juice, oil, vanilla, and walnuts and mix together gently until "just mixed". Spoon into a lightly oiled 20x20cm/8x8in tin and bake for 25-30 minutes. Test with a knife to see if done. **Makes 6 large brownies.**

# CHOCOLATE PECAN BROWNIES

Whoever thought a vegan dessert could ever be so rich and decadent? Try this tantalizing confection and chide yourself for ever thinking vegan baking was dull. This and the brownie recipe on pg.127 will test the most critical sweet-tooth's palate.

225g/8oz soft or medium tofu

200g/7oz dry sweetener

2 teaspoons vanilla extract

4 tablespoons oil

4 tablespoons cocoa or carob powder

165g/5½ oz wholemeal pastry flour

2 teaspoons baking powder

75g/3oz pecans, chopped

Preheat oven to 180°C/350°F/gas mark 4. In a blender or food processor, blend the tofu, sweetener, vanilla, oil, and cocoa powder until smooth and creamy. In a large bowl, sift together the flour and baking powder. Add the pecans and tofu mixture, and mix together gently until "just mixed". If the batter is too dry, add a splash of water. Spoon the batter into a lightly oiled 20x20cm/8x8in cake tin and bake for 20-25 minutes. Test with a knife to see if done. Let cool in tin for 5 minutes before icing (pg. 143) and cutting into squares. **Makes 6 large brownies.**

# CHOCOLATE PEANUT BUTTER CUPS

For years, the idea of making your own peanut butter cups seemed a laborious task. Now thanks to the efforts of vegan pioneers, recipes like this are only a little harder than making ice cubes.

115g/4oz margarine

175g/6oz peanut butter or other nut butter (e.g., cashew)

40g/1½ oz digestive biscuit crumbs

4 tablespoons dry sweetener

175g/6oz chocolate or carob chips

4 tablespoons soy milk

4 tablespoons nuts, chopped

12 paper cake cases

In a small saucepan on medium heat, melt the margarine. Once liquefied, stir in the peanut butter, biscuit crumbs, and sweetener until well incorporated. Spoon about 2 tablespoons of the peanut mixture into muffin tins lined with paper cake cases (the cases are important). In a different small saucepan on medium heat, melt the chocolate and milk together until completely melted, stirring often. Spoon over top of the peanut butter cups. Garnish with nuts and allow to set in the fridge for 6-8 hours before serving. **Makes 12 cupcakes.**

# CHOCOLATE RICE CRISPY SQUARES

Children and adults of all ages will appreciate this crispy, sticky, taste sensation.

200g/7oz dry sweetener
250ml/8fl oz golden syrup
225g/8oz peanut butter or nut butter

175g/6oz puffed rice or other puffed grain
350g/12oz chocolate or carob chips

In small saucepan on medium heat, mix together the sweetener and golden syrup until hot and bubbly. Remove from heat and add the nut butter, stirring together until well mixed. In a large bowl, add the puffed rice and chips. Stir in the nut butter mixture and mix together well. Pour mixture into a 23x33cm/9x13in tin, press flat, and let cool for 1 hour before cutting into squares. **Makes 6 large or 12 small squares.**

# CHOCOLATE CHIP BARS

Please, oh please lock me up so I can eat my way to freedom, straight through these fantastic chocolate chip bars. **T**

400g/14oz plain flour
1 1/2 teaspoons baking powder
1/2 teaspoon bicarbonate of soda
1/2 teaspoon salt
300g/11oz dry sweetener

250ml/8fl oz oil
1 teaspoon vanilla extract
250ml/8fl oz soy milk or water
175g/6oz chocolate or carob chips

Preheat oven to 180°C/350°F/gas mark 4. In a large bowl, stir together the flour, baking powder, bicarbonate of soda, salt, and sweetener. Add the oil, vanilla, milk, and chocolate chips and mix together gently until "just mixed". Pour mixture into a 23x33cm/9x13in tin and bake for 25-30 minutes. Test with a knife to see if done. Let cool 10 minutes before cutting into bars. **Makes 12 bars.**

# MAPLE NUT ORBS

Absolutely delicious. A healthy treat requiring only a few ingredients. You'll make these often! For chocolate orbs, add 50g/2oz cocoa powder to the dough.

225g/8oz nut butter (e.g., peanut, cashew, tahini)
75-125ml/2 1/2-4fl oz maple syrup
115g/4oz oat bran

75g/3oz wheatgerm
225g/8oz sesame seeds
40g/1 1/2 oz desiccated coconut

In a food processor, blend together the nut butter and maple syrup. Add the oat bran, wheatgerm, and sesame seeds and blend until it has a stiff, dough-like consistency. You can either roll the dough into 14 individual orbs, and then roll them in coconut and chill, or spread the dough onto a square pan and sprinkle with coconut, chill, and cut into squares. **Makes 14 orbs.**

# DELIGHTFUL DATE SQUARES

Also known as the "matrimonial square", this recipe overflows with wholesome goodness, given the oats and the dates, which are full of iron. Date squares are a prestigious confection perfect for those unexpected occasions when royalty comes a knocking.

**Filling:**
250ml/8fl oz water
350g/12oz pitted dates, chopped
1/2 teaspoon salt

**Crust:**
350g/12oz rolled oat flakes
225g/8oz plain flour

200g/7oz dry sweetener
1/2 teaspoon salt
1/2 teaspoon baking powder
1/2 teaspoon bicarbonate of soda
1 teaspoon cinnamon
225g/8oz margarine
4 tablespoons oil
4 tablespoons water (optional)

Preheat oven to 180°C/350°F/gas mark 4. In a small saucepan, bring the water to boil, then reduce to medium heat and add the dates and 1/2 a teaspoon of the salt, and simmer until the dates are soft and will mix easily with the water. Remove from heat and set aside to cool.

In a large bowl, stir together the oat flakes, flour, sweetener, salt, baking powder, bicarbonate of soda, and cinnamon. Add the margarine and oil and stir together until well combined. If the crust is too dry, add the optional water.

Press half of the crust mixture into the bottom of a 23x33cm/9x13in tin. Spread the date mixture over top, spreading out with the back of a large spoon. Sprinkle the remaining crust mixture over top. Bake for 25-40 minutes, until the top is lightly browned and tender. Crust will harden when it cools, so cut into squares before it gets too difficult! **Makes 12 bars.**

# MUESLI BARS

115g/4oz muesli (pg. 45)
75g/3oz desiccated coconut, shredded
90g/3 1/2 oz rolled oat flakes
115g/4oz plain flour
3/4 teaspoon baking powder
pinch of salt

90g/3 1/2 oz sweetener
65g/2 1/2 oz raisins
flax or psyllium egg replacer (to equal 1 egg)
125ml/4fl oz oil
2 tablespoons sesame seeds

Preheat oven to 180°C/350°F/gas mark 4. In a large bowl stir together the muesli, coconut, oat flakes, flour, baking powder, and salt. Stir in the sweetener, raisins, egg replacer, and oil. Mix together well. Spread mixture into a 20x20cm/8x8in tin. Sprinkle top evenly with sesame seeds. Bake for 18-20 minutes.

# GINGER SNAPS

This temptation was Hansel and Gretel's downfall. But fear not, these snaps hold no hidden traps. No need to proceed gingerly!

275g/10oz plain flour
1 teaspoon baking powder
1 teaspoon bicarbonate of soda
1/2 teaspoon salt

175ml/6fl oz maple syrup
4 tablespoons molasses
125ml/4fl oz oil
5 tablespoons fresh ginger, grated

Preheat oven to 180°C/350°F/gas mark 4. In a large bowl, stir together the flour, baking powder, bicarbonate of soda, and salt. Add the maple syrup, molasses, oil, and ginger. Stir together gently until "just mixed". Scoop spoon-sized portions onto a lightly oiled baking sheet and bake for 12-15 minutes. **Makes 6 large or 12 small cookies.**

# CLASSIC CHOCOLATE CHIP COOKIES

A vegan version of the kind of cookies that Grandma used to make. Serve with a big cold glass of soy milk.

150g/5oz dry sweetener
115g/4oz margarine
125ml/4fl oz oil
3 tablespoons water
2 teaspoons vanilla extract

250g/9oz plain flour
1 teaspoon bicarbonate of soda
1/2 teaspoon salt
175-250g/6-9oz chocolate chips

Preheat oven to 190°C/375°F/gas mark 5. In a small bowl, stir together the sweetener, margarine, oil, water, and vanilla. In a large bowl, mix together the flour, bicarbonate of soda, and salt. Add the margarine mixture and the chocolate chips and mix together well. Scoop spoon-sized portions onto an unoiled baking sheet and bake for 8-10 minutes or until the edges are browned. Let cool before removing from baking sheet. **Makes 6 large or 12 small cookies.**

# BANANA OATMEAL COOKIES

These oatmeal cookies are no plain jane treats. In fact, their sensation is in their subtlety.

2 bananas, mashed
115g/4oz apple sauce
90g/3½ oz dry sweetener
1 teaspoon vanilla extract
275g/10oz plain flour

225g/8oz rolled oat flakes
1 teaspoon cinnamon
1 teaspoon bicarbonate of soda
150g/5oz raisins
75g/3oz chocolate or carob chips

Preheat oven to 180°C/350°F/gas mark 4. In a food processor or small bowl, mix together the bananas, apple sauce, sweetener, and vanilla. In large bowl, stir together the flour, oat flakes, cinnamon, and bicarbonate of soda. Add the banana mixture and mix together well. Add the raisins and chips and mix together again. Scoop spoon-sized portions onto a lightly oiled baking sheet and bake for 12-15 minutes. **Makes 6 large or 12 small cookies.**

# SPICY OATMEAL RAISIN COOKIES

Delicately flavoured with herbs and spices, the uniqueness of these cookies intrigues all.

275g/10oz rolled oat flakes
115g/4oz plain flour
½ teaspoon salt
1 teaspoon bicarbonate of soda
1 teaspoon cinnamon
1 teaspoon nutmeg
1 teaspoon ground ginger
1 teaspoon cumin
½ teaspoon dried cardamom

½ teaspoon pepper
dash of cayenne pepper
1 banana, mashed
90g/3½ oz dry sweetener
2 tablespoons oil
250ml/8fl oz sour soy milk (soy milk plus 1 teaspoon vinegar)
115g/4oz raisins
75g/3oz chocolate or carob chips (optional)

Preheat oven to 190°C/375°F/gas mark 5. In a large bowl, stir together the oat flakes, flour, salt, bicarbonate of soda, cinnamon, nutmeg, ginger, cumin, cardamom, pepper, and cayenne pepper. Add the mashed banana, sweetener, oil, sour milk, raisins, and chocolate chips to the oat mixture and mix together gently until "just mixed". Scoop spoon-sized portions onto a lightly oiled baking sheet and bake for 8-10 minutes. **Makes 6 large or 12 small cookies.**

# APRICOT & ALMOND TEA COOKIES

Truly delectable. An elegant cookie suitable for all occasions.

225g/8oz plain flour
3/4 teaspoon baking powder
1/2 teaspoon bicarbonate of soda
1/2 teaspoon salt
115g/4oz rolled oat flakes
90g/3 1/2 oz sweetener

115g/4oz almonds, chopped
115g/4oz dried apricots, chopped
125ml/4fl oz oil
4 tablespoons soy milk
1 tablespoon vanilla extract

Preheat oven to 180°C/350°F/gas mark 4. In a large bowl, sift together the flour, baking powder, bicarbonate of soda, and salt. Add the oat flakes, sweetener, almonds, apricots, oil, milk, and vanilla. If the mixture is too dry, add a splash of water (but you don't want them gooey). Scoop spoon-sized portions onto a lightly oiled baking sheet and bake for 12-15 minutes. **Makes 12 large or 24 small cookies.**

# AUNTIE BONNIE'S KAMISH BREAD COOKIES

These cookies are a Kramer family favourite that we've adapted. They freeze well and are great for tea parties or munching when you're feeling nibbly. **S**

6 tablespoons cane sugar
1/2 teaspoon cinnamon
275g/10oz plain flour
90g/3 1/2 oz dry sweetener
1 teaspoon baking powder
dash of salt
150g/5oz apple sauce or
    egg replacer (to equal 3 eggs)

4 tablespoons oil
1 teaspoon vanilla extract
115g/4oz almonds, chopped
4 tablespoons desiccated coconut
4 tablespoons  chocolate or carob chips

Preheat oven to 180°C/350°F/gas mark 4. In a small bowl, mix together the cane sugar and cinnamon and set aside. In a large bowl, whisk together the flour, sweetener, baking powder, and salt. Add in the apple sauce, oil, vanilla, almonds, coconut, and chips and mix together gently until "just mixed". Separate the dough into 3 balls. Cover your baking sheet with foil, then roll each ball into a snake shape the length of the baking sheet.

Press down a little so the dough is about an inch thick. Repeat with the remaining balls of dough. Sprinkle each log with the cinnamon-sugar mixture. Bake for 35-40 minutes. Before cookies cool, cut each log into 24 slices. Place cookies back on the baking sheet and bake for another hour at 100°C/200°F/gas mark 1/4. **Makes 72 small cookies.**

# COOTIE'S COCONUT COOKIES

These are best straight from the oven, but they're nice and chewy when cold, too.

2 bananas, mashed
1 teaspoon vanilla extract
90g/3¹/₂ oz sweetener
125ml/4fl oz oil
3 teaspoons coconut or soy milk

115g/4oz plain flour
1 teaspoon bicarbonate of soda
1 teaspoon cinnamon
90g/3¹/₂ oz rolled oat flakes
75g/3oz coconut, shredded

Preheat oven to 180°C/350°F/gas mark 4. In a blender or food processor, blend together the mashed bananas, vanilla, sweetener, oil, and milk. In a large bowl, sift together the flour, bicarbonate of soda, and cinnamon. Stir in the oat flakes and then fold in the banana mixture, stirring well. Mix in the desiccated coconut. Scoop spoon-sized portions onto a lightly oiled baking sheet and bake for 15-20 minutes. **Makes 12 large or 24 small cookies.**

# HOT WATER PIE CRUST

Does the filling make the pie, or is it the crust? After all, the crust is the foundation that holds this classic dessert together. Without it, it's just jam.

225g/8oz vegetable shortening
1 teaspoon margarine
175ml/6fl oz boiling water

400g/14oz pastry flour or 350g/12oz plain flour*
2 tablespoons baking powder
1/4 teaspoon salt

In a large bowl, mix together the shortening, margarine, and water until creamy. Add the flour, baking powder, and salt and mix together until a dough forms. Knead for a minute or two. Wrap the dough in greaseproof paper and chill for about 3 hours before rolling it out (not overnight). Roll the dough into individual pie crusts. **Makes 2 crusts.**

If you want to freeze the dough to use later, roll out to the size you want and place in an airtight container, placing a sheet of greaseproof paper between the sheets of dough. Fold the sheets as necessary to fit in the container, but thaw completely before unfolding and using for pie. When ready to use, bake at 180°C/350°F/gas mark 4 for 15 minutes and let cool before adding filling.

*Note: white flour works better than wholemeal flour for pie crusts. You lose some nutrition, but live a little!

# SOURDOUGH PIE CRUST

This is a versatile crust. Use with your favourite fruit filling.

115g/4oz plain flour
1/2 teaspoon salt
1/4 teaspoon bicarbonate of soda

75g/3oz vegetable shortening or margarine
5 tablespoons sourdough starter (pg. 115)

In a large bowl, sift together the flour, salt, and bicarbonate of soda. Cut the shortening into the flour mixture and, once well-mixed, add the sourdough starter and stir together well. Set bowl aside and let dough rise, covered, for about half an hour. Roll the dough into a pie crust. **Makes 1 crust.**

# DIGESTIVE BISCUIT CRUST

Use this with the "cheese" cake recipes (pg. 139-140).

75g/3oz digestive biscuit crumbs
2-3 tablespoons oil

3 tablespoons water
dash of salt

In a medium bowl, mix together all the ingredients. Press the mixture evenly onto the bottom of a pie plate or cheesecake pan, using your fingers or the back of a spoon. **Makes 1 crust.**

# ROLLED OAT PIE CRUST

This crust is good for apple pie, or in place of the digestive biscuit crust.

185g/6 1/2 oz rolled oat flakes
50g/2oz vegetable shortening or margarine

90g/3 1/2 oz sweetener
1/4 teaspoon cinnamon

In a medium bowl, mix together all the ingredients. Press the mixture evenly onto the bottom of a pie plate or cheesecake pan, using your fingers or the back of a spoon. Bake at 180°C/350°F/gas mark 4 for 10 minutes before using. **Makes 1 crust.**

# AMAZING APPLE PIE

Just imagine this hot pie cooling on your window sill, brimming with raisins and apples, with a slight hint of maple. It makes a fabulous team with vanilla ice cream (pg.148) when served oven-hot. You can add any other fruit combinations. Just subtract 1 apple for each 115g/4oz of fruit.

6-8 large cooking apples (Granny Smith are best), cored and sliced

65g/2¹/2 oz raisins (optional)

175ml/6fl oz maple syrup

1-2 tablespoons lemon juice

2 teaspoons cinnamon

2¹/2 tablespoons cornflour or arrowroot powder

1 pie crust (pgs. 134-135)

Preheat oven to 180°C/350°F/gas mark 4. Core and slice apples into bite-sized pieces. Bring a medium pan of water to boil, then reduce heat to medium and add the apples and optional raisins to simmer for 8-10 minutes. Save 4 tablespoons of "apple water" for use later. Drain apples and place in a large bowl. Mix carefully together the cooked apples, maple syrup, lemon juice, and cinnamon. Set aside. In a small saucepan, mix the 4 tablespoons "apple water" with the cornflour over medium heat, stirring constantly until the mixture turns very thick. Add the cornflour mixture to the rest of the ingredients, stirring until mixed well. Pour into a pie crust and bake for 30-40 minutes.

Note: If you're too busy to make a pie crust, there are shop-bought crusts available that are vegan. Just check the ingredients.

# PERFECT PUMPKIN PIE

Pumpkin, or winter squash, is usually harvested in the autumn, just in time for winter solstice and other seasonal holidays. Which is why this pie always makes its way to the table alongside the tofu turkey (pg. 110). This delicious old favourite is sure to be a hit, especially when topped with whipped cream (pg. 145).

350ml/12fl oz soy milk

egg replacer (to equal 2 eggs)

1 x 450g can pumpkin

125ml/4fl oz sweetener

1 teaspoon cinnamon

1/2 teaspoon ground ginger

1 pie crust (pgs. 134-135 )

Preheat oven to 180°C/350°F/gas mark 4. In a large bowl, whisk together the milk and the egg replacer. Add the pumpkin, sweetener, cinnamon, and ginger, and mix together well. Pour into a pie crust and bake for 30-40 minutes, until centre is firm.

# CREAMY COCONUT PIE

Classically creamy and light as a cloud, this is the kind of pie dreams are made of.

450g/1lb soft tofu
125ml/4fl oz oil
2 teaspoons vanilla extract
1/2 teaspoon salt

300g/11 oz dry sweetener
175g/6oz desiccated coconut
1 digestive biscuit pie crust (pg. 135)

Preheat oven to 180°C/350°F/gas mark 4. In a blender or food processor, blend together the tofu, oil, vanilla, salt, and sweetener. Pour into a large bowl and fold in 275g/10oz of the coconut. Pour into a digestive biscuit pie crust and bake for 15 minutes. Sprinkle the remaining coconut on top and bake for another 10 minutes, until filling looks set and centre is firm. Serve chilled.

# CHOCOLATE BOURBON PECAN PIE

Formally referred to as the "orgasm pie". One bite and you will understand. This pie is so elegant and rich, it has a reputation. Three words describe it: "better than sex!"

egg replacer (to equal two eggs)
2 tablespoons molasses
125ml/4fl oz golden syrup
2 tablespoons Jack Daniels bourbon (optional)
1 teaspoon vanilla extract

1/8 teaspoon salt
175g/6oz pecans, chopped
175g/6oz chocolate chips
4 whole pecans
1 pie crust (pgs. 134-135)

Preheat oven to 180°C/350°F/gas mark 4. In a large bowl, mix together the egg replacer, molasses, golden syrup, bourbon, vanilla, and salt. Add the chopped pecans and chocolate chips and mix together well. Pour into a pie crust and arrange the 4 whole pecans in the centre of the pie as decoration. Bake for 40-45 minutes.

# CHOCOLATE-BANANA NO-BAKE PIE

No-bake pie! Sounds crazy, you say? Try it, we say.

175g/6oz  chocolate chips
splash of soy milk
300g/11oz apple sauce

90g/3¹/₂ oz dry sweetener
4 bananas, chopped
1 pie crust (pgs.134-135)

In a small double boiler, melt the chocolate chips with a splash of milk over hot water, stirring until smooth.

In a blender or food processor, blend together the apple sauce, sweetener, bananas, and melted chocolate until well mixed. Pour into the pie crust of your choice. Chill for at least 12 hours before eating.

# ANGELIC APPLE CRISP

If there is a heaven, it will have the aroma of baked apples. If heaven has a restaurant, it will serve this apple crisp recipe. Since we're not in heaven yet, we might as well eat as if we are. This recipe is best with ice cream (pg.148-149).

6-8 apples, cored and chopped
40-75g/1¹/₂-3oz raisins (optional)
5 tablespoons apple juice
125ml/4fl oz maple syrup

**Topping:**
90g/3¹/₂ oz rolled oat flakes
50g/2oz plain flour
50g/2oz margarine
50g/2oz sweetener
¹/₂-1 teaspoon cinnamon
¹/₂ teaspoon ground ginger
dash of salt
dash of nutmeg
25-50g/1-2oz chopped nuts (optional)

Preheat oven to 180°C/350°F/gas mark 4. Core and chop the apples into bite-sized pieces. Place onto a lightly oiled baking dish and mix in the optional raisins. In a small bowl, mix together the juice and maple syrup. Pour the juice mixture over the apples and raisins evenly. In a medium bowl, mix together the oat flakes, flour, margarine, sweetener, cinnamon, ginger, salt, nutmeg, and optional nuts. Sprinkle the oat mixture over top of apples and bake for 30-40 minutes.
**Makes 4-6 servings.**

# APPLE CINNAMON MATZO KUGEL

A lovely variation on an old favourite. Imagine small morsels of apple flawlessly baked, combined with fragments of pecans, raisins, and matzos. Serve with banana vanilla ice cream (pg.148).

4 matzos
4 tablespoons oil
egg replacer (to equal 3 eggs)
90g/3¹/₂ oz sweetener
¹/₂ teaspoon salt

1 teaspoon cinnamon
50g/2oz pecans, chopped
65g/2¹/₂ oz raisins
2-3 apples, cored and chopped

Preheat oven to 180°C/350°F/gas mark 4. Break matzos into quarters and soak in a medium bowl of water until soft. Drain, but do not squeeze dry. In a medium casserole dish, mix together the oil, egg replacer, sweetener, salt, and cinnamon. Stir in the matzos, pecans, raisins, and apples. Bake for 45 minutes. **Makes 4-6 servings.**

# CHOCOLATE "CHEESE" CAKE

Chocolate lovers beware. This dessert is truly magical.

675g/1¹/₂ lb medium tofu
225g/8oz margarine, melted
200-300g/7-11oz dry sweetener
90g/3¹/₂ oz cocoa powder

2 teaspoons vanilla extract
¹/₄ teaspoon salt
125ml/4fl oz soy milk
1 digestive biscuit pie crust (pg.135)

In a blender or food processor, blend all the ingredients until smooth. Pour into a cheesecake tin that has been lined with a digestive biscuit crust. Chill for at least 12 hours before eating.

# PINEAPPLE "CHEESE" CAKE

This cheesecake has just the right amount of pineapple zing. Garnish with fresh fruit sauce (pg. 146) or fresh fruit slices.

500g/1¼ lb silken tofu
450g/1lb medium tofu
lemon zest from 1 lemon
1½ teaspoons lemon juice
120ml4fl oz golden syrup
90g/3½ oz dry sweetener

2 tablespoons oil
2½ teaspoons vanilla extract
dash of salt
115g/4oz pineapple, finely chopped
1 digestive biscuit pie crust (pg.135)

Preheat oven to 160°C/325°F/gas mark 3. In a blender or food processor, blend the tofus, lemon zest, lemon juice, golden syrup, sweetener, oil, vanilla, and salt until very smooth. Stir in the pineapple and pour into a cheesecake tin that has been lined with a digestive biscuit crust. Bake for 45-60 minutes until centre is well-set and a knife inserted into the centre comes out clean. Serve chilled.

# JEN'S CHOCOLATE CAKE

Cake making has never been so easy. Crown with any delicious icing recipe from pgs. 143-144.

350g/12oz plain flour
2 teaspoons bicarbonate of soda
½ teaspoon salt
90g/3½ oz cocoa powder
175g/6oz margarine

300g/11oz dry sweetener
4 tablespoons water
475ml/16fl oz soy milk
2 teaspoons vanilla extract

Preheat oven to 180°C/350°F/gas mark 4. In a large bowl, stir together the flour, bicarbonate of soda, salt, and cocoa powder. In a blender or food processor, blend together the margarine, sweetener, and water. Add this to flour mixture along with the milk and vanilla, and mix together gently until "just mixed". Pour into a lightly oiled 20cm/8in cake tin and bake for 30 minutes. Test with a fork to see if done. When cooled, ice and serve.

# AUNTIE BONNIE'S WACKY CAKE

A mouth-watering surprise. Perfect for birthdays, anniversaries, or any special occasion. And yup, that's vinegar in the list of ingredients.

175g/6oz plain flour
4 tablespoons cocoa or carob powder
1 teaspoon baking powder
1 teaspoon bicarbonate of soda
1/2 teaspoon salt

200g/7oz dry sweetener
1 1/2 teaspoons vanilla extract
1 tablespoon vinegar
5 tablespoons oil
250ml/8fl oz cold water

Preheat oven to 160°C/325°F/gas mark 3. In a large bowl, stir together the flour, cocoa powder, baking powder, bicarbonate of soda, and salt. Add the sweetener, vanilla, vinegar, oil, and water and mix together gently until "just mixed". Pour into a lightly oiled 20cm/8in cake tin and bake for 45-50 minutes. Test with a fork to see if done. When cooled, ice (pgs.143-144) and serve.

# VANILLA CAKE

These next two cakes are just the right dessert to top off a great meal. A light, airy cake with the essence of vanilla or lemon.

175g/6oz plain flour
2 teaspoons baking powder
1/4 teaspoon salt
90g/3 1/2 oz dry sweetener

175ml/6fl oz soy milk
2 teaspoons vanilla extract
4 tablespoons oil
egg replacer (to equal 1 egg)

Preheat oven to 180°C/350°F/gas mark 4. In a large bowl, stir together the flour, baking powder, and salt. Add the sweetener, milk, vanilla, oil, and egg replacer and mix together gently until "just mixed". Pour into a lightly oiled 20cm/8in cake tin and bake for 25-30 minutes. Check with a knife to see if done. When cooled, ice (pgs. 143-144) and serve.

# LEMON CAKE

175g/6oz plain flour
2 teaspoons baking powder
1/4 teaspoon salt
150g/5oz dry sweetener
175ml/6fl oz soy milk

2 teaspoons lemon extract
zest of 1 lemon
4 tablespoons oil
egg replacer (to equal 1 egg)

Preheat oven to 180°C/350°F/gas mark 4. In a large bowl, stir together the flour, baking powder, and salt. Add the sweetener, milk, lemon extract, lemon zest, oil, and egg replacer and mix together gently until "just mixed". Pour into a lightly oiled 20cm/8in cake tin and bake for 25-30 minutes. Check with a knife to see if done. When cooled, ice (pgs.143-144) and serve.

# COUNTRY CARROT CAKE

No one will ever know that this vegan version of an all-time classic is so easy to prepare.

175g/6oz plain flour
150g/5oz dry sweetener
2 teaspoons baking powder
1 teaspoon cinnamon
1/4 teaspoon salt
175ml/6fl oz soy milk

2 teaspoons vanilla extract
4 tablespoons oil
egg replacer (to equal 1 egg)
65g/2 1/2 oz carrot, finely shredded
1 teaspoon fresh ginger, grated

Preheat oven to 180°C/350°F/gas mark 4. In a large bowl, stir together the flour, sweetener, baking powder, cinnamon, and salt. Add the milk, vanilla, oil, egg replacer, carrot, and ginger and mix together gently until "just mixed". Pour into a lightly oiled 20cm/8in cake tin and bake for 25-30 minutes. Check with a knife to see if done. When cooled, ice with To-Fruity Cream Cheese (pg. 82) and serve.

# CHOCOLATE UPSIDE DOWN PUDDING CAKE

Don't let the name fool you. Is it a cake, is it pudding? It's just good!

115g/4oz plain flour
1 tablespoon baking powder
25g/1oz cocoa powder
1/4 teaspoon salt
90g/3 1/2 oz dry sweetener
115g/4oz margarine
125ml/4fl oz soy milk
1 teaspoon vanilla extract

Sauce:
150g/5oz dry sweetener
25g/1oz cocoa powder
475ml/16fl oz boiling water

Preheat oven to 180°C/350°F/gas mark 4. In a large bowl, stir together the flour, baking powder, cocoa, and salt. Add the sweetener, margarine, milk, and vanilla and mix together gently until "just mixed". Spread in a lightly oiled casserole dish or loaf tin. Set aside.

In a medium bowl, mix together the sweetener and cocoa. Sprinkle evenly on top of the cake mixture. Carefully pour the boiling water over top. Note: DO NOT MIX THIS! It will do its own thing in the oven. Bake for 40 minutes. To serve, scoop out portions and serve in a bowl with ice cream (pg. 148).

The recipes for these icings are enough to ice 1 layer of a cake or 6 cupcakes.

# CHOCOLATE ICING

This icing is the perfect finishing touch – velvety and oh-so-smooth.

250ml/8fl oz cold water
5 tablespoons plain flour
200g/7oz dry sweetener

1 teaspoon vanilla extract
6 tablespoons margarine
3 tablespoons cocoa powder

In a small saucepan, whisk together the water and flour constantly over medium heat until thick (about the consistency of glue). Be careful not to burn it! Once thick, remove from heat and cool off completely by setting the pot in a slightly larger pan of cold water, or a sink with a bit of cold water. While it's cooling, in a medium bowl, mix together the sweetener, vanilla, margarine, and cocoa powder until well mixed. Add the cooled flour mixture to the bowl and stir together until there are no lumps. Let cool in the fridge for 30-60 minutes – before using.

# COFFEE ICING

A grown-up tasting sweet treat.

450g/1lb medium tofu
90g/3 1/2 oz dry sweetener
4 tablespoons oil

2 teaspoons vanilla extract
2-3 tablespoons coffee or Inka
dash of salt

In a blender or food processor blend all the ingredients together until well mixed. Pour into a medium bowl and chill for at least 2 hours before using.

# NUT BUTTER ICING

A scrumptious topping that is Sarah's favourite.

3 tablespoons margarine
90g/3 1/2 oz dry sweetener
65g/2 1/2 oz peanut butter (or other nut butter)

2 tablespoons soy milk
40g/1 1/2 oz nuts, chopped (optional)

In a medium bowl or food processor, mix together the margarine, sweetener, and nut butter. Add the milk and mix well. Stir in nuts before using.

# MAPLE BUTTERESQUE ICING

This icing is a dazzler. A decadent way to top any cake.

115g/4oz margarine
350g/12oz icing sugar*

6 tablespoons maple syrup
25g/1oz walnuts or pecans, chopped

In a medium bowl, thoroughly mix together the margarine and sugar. Stir in the maple syrup until consistency is light and spreadable. Stir in nuts before using.

# MARVELLOUS MAPLE ICING

A perfect icing for your perfect cake.

50g/2oz margarine
250g/9oz icing sugar*

2 tablespoons soy milk
1 teaspoon maple syrup

In a food processor or medium bowl, mix together the margarine and 115g/4oz of the icing sugar. Add remaining sugar alternately with milk, mixing until smooth. Stir in the maple syrup until consistency is light and spreadable.

# "ANYTHING GOES" ICING

A versatile classic. Vary the colour for each occasion.

50g/2oz margarine
250g/9oz icing sugar*
2 tablespoons soy milk

1 teaspoon flavouring extract of your choice e.g.,
lemon, peppermint, or maple

In a food processor or medium bowl, mix together the margarine with 115g/4oz of the icing sugar. Add remaining sugar alternately with milk, mixing until smooth. Stir in the extract until consistency is light and spreadable.

*You can make icing sugar yourself by blending sugar in a dry blender or food processor until finely ground.

# SOY MILK WHIPPED CREAM

And you thought you'd never get to eat anything this scrumptious again.

4 tablespoons soy milk

2-4 tablespoons sweetener

1/2 teaspoon vanilla extract

1 teaspoon cornflour

125ml/4fl oz oil

In a blender or food processor, blend together the milk, sweetener, vanilla, and cornflour. Slowly drizzle in the oil while the blender is running. Blend until smooth and creamy. Chill for 1 hour before using. **Makes approx. 175ml/6fl oz.**

# TOFU WHIPPED CREAM

A light and satisfying dessert topping.

350g/12oz soft tofu

2-4 tablespoons sweetener

2 teaspoons vanilla extract

2 teaspoons cornflour

In a blender or food processor, blend all the ingredients well. Chill for 1 hour before using. **Makes approx. 250ml/8fl oz.**

# BANANA-RAMA CREAM

Enjoy this rich, creamy sauce over fruit salad, oatmeal, even pancakes.

1 banana, chopped

2 tablespoons oil

1 teaspoon vanilla extract

1/2 teaspoon lemon juice

In a blender or food processor, blend together the banana, oil, vanilla, and lemon juice until smooth and creamy. Use immediately. Add a little water if you want to thin it out a bit. **Makes approx. 175ml/6fl oz.**

# CASHEW CREAM

Use this as a creamy topping for fruit, puddings, or cake.

50g/2oz raw cashews
250ml/8fl oz white grape juice
1/4 teaspoon vanilla extract

In a blender or food processor, finely grind the cashew nuts. Add the grape juice and vanilla and blend together until smooth and creamy. Strain out any lumps and chill. **Makes approx. 175ml/ 6fl oz.**

# FRESH FRUIT SAUCE

A fruit-filled version of a cool favourite.

225g/8oz fresh fruit (e.g., blueberries, strawberries)
5 tablespoons maple syrup

In a blender or food processor, blend together 175g/6oz of the fruit and maple syrup until saucy. Pour into a medium bowl and stir in the remaining fruit. Spoon over dessert. **Makes approx. 125ml/4fl oz.**

# SINFUL CHOCOLATE PUDDING

Chocolate lovers take note. Bask in the most delicious of chocolate treats.

225g/8oz soft tofu
4 tablespoons oil
90g/3 1/2 oz sweetener

4 tablespoons cocoa powder
1/4 teaspoon salt
1 1/2 teaspoons vanilla extract

In a blender or food processor, blend together all the ingredients until smooth and creamy. Chill well before serving. **Makes 2-4 servings.**

# CREAMY BANANA PUDDING

Delicate banana flavouring accents this creamy dessert.

225g/8oz soft tofu
2 bananas, chopped
3 tablespoons dates, chopped (optional)
2¹/₂ tablespoons oil

50g/2oz sweetener
1 teaspoon lemon juice
dash of salt
1/2 teaspoon vanilla extract

In a blender or food processor, blend together all the ingredients until smooth and creamy. Chill well before serving. **Makes 2-4 servings.**

# "ANYTHING GOES" FRUIT PUDDING

A dessert spectacular. Create any combination you wish.

225g/8oz soft tofu
2¹/₂ tablespoons oil
50g/2oz sweetener
dash of salt

75g/3oz fresh or frozen fruit of your choice
1/2 teaspoon vanilla extract
1/2 teaspoon lemon juice

In a blender or food processor, blend together all the ingredients until smooth and creamy. Chill well before serving. **Makes 2-4 servings.**

# CHOCOLATE ICE CREAM

Enjoy this old time favourite, then watch how everyone screams for more ice cream.

450g/1lb soft tofu
250ml/8fl oz soy milk
125ml/4fl oz oil
90-200g/3¹/₂-7oz dry sweetener

25g/1oz cocoa powder
1 tablespoon vanilla extract
dash of salt

In a food processor, blend together all the ingredients until very smooth and creamy. Place in a sealable container and freeze. Remove from freezer and defrost for 20-40 minutes. Place back in food processor and blend again. Spoon back into container (at this point, you may add chocolate chips or crumbled biscuits if you like), then re-freeze. Remove from freezer 5 minutes before serving. **Makes 4-6 servings.**

# VANILLA BANANA ICE CREAM

Rich, flavourful, and easy to make.

225g/8oz soft tofu
250ml/8fl oz soy milk
125ml/4fl oz oil
2 bananas, chopped

65g/2¹/₂ oz dry sweetener
2 tablespoons lemon juice
1¹/₂ tablespoons vanilla extract
dash of salt

In a food processor, blend together all the ingredients until very smooth and creamy. Place in a sealable container and freeze. Remove from freezer and defrost for 20-40 minutes. Place back in food processor and blend again. Spoon back into container and re-freeze. Remove from freezer 5 minutes before serving. **Makes 4-6 servings.**

# "ANYTHING GOES" FRUITY ICE CREAM

Use whatever fruit you'd like with this — strawberries, blueberries, peaches...

450g/1lb soft tofu
125ml/4fl oz soy milk
125ml/4fl oz oil
200g/7oz dry sweetener

1 tablespoon lemon juice
175g/6oz fresh or frozen fruit of your choice
1 tablespoon vanilla extract
dash of salt

In a food processor, combine all the ingredients except for 50g/2oz of the fruit, and blend together until very smooth and creamy. Place in a sealable container and freeze. Remove from freezer and defrost for 20-40 minutes. Place back in food processor and blend again. Spoon back into container and add the remaining fruit. Re-freeze. Remove from freezer 5 minutes before serving. **Makes 4-6 servings.**

# COFFEE ICE CREAM

A creamy, delicious blend.

4 tablespoons soy milk
5 tablespoons oil
1 banana, chopped

50g/2oz sweetener
2-3 teaspoons instant coffee powder or Inka grain
   beverage

In a food processor, blend together all the ingredients until very smooth and creamy. Place in a sealable container and freeze. Remove from freezer and defrost for 20-40 minutes. Place back in food processor and blend again. Spoon back into container and re-freeze. Remove from freezer 5 minutes before serving. **Makes 4-6 servings.**

Check out pages 172-173 for other fantastic frozen treats!

# VEGAN ODDS
# & SODS

This is a collection of wonderful and flavourful recipes that just didn't seem to fit anywhere else in this book, but that doesn't make them any less great. Included here are condiments, dips, spicy and savoury toppings, and healthy snacks. Fearlessly indulge yourself in the exotica of vegan miscellany!

# FLAX EGGS

Flax eggs are great as a binder in pancakes, breads, and other baking, but not to eat on their own. 3 tablespoons of flax eggs equals 1 egg.

5 tablespoons whole flax seeds
250ml/8fl oz water

In a blender or food processor, blend the seeds until finely ground. Then slowly add water while blending. Blend until mixture resembles a thick milkshake. Transfer to a sealable container and store in the fridge (will keep for 3-6 days). If you like you can pour through a sieve to remove seeds. **Makes the equivalent of 6 eggs.**

# SOY MILK MAYONNAISE

One of the greatest challenges facing vegans is having to abstain from that fantastic creamy condiment known as mayonnaise. But fear not: it's time to welcome mayonnaise back into your life.

175ml/6fl oz soy milk
1 1/2 tablespoons lemon juice or vinegar
3/4 teaspoon salt

dash of pepper
175ml/6fl oz oil

In a blender or food processor, blend together (on high) the milk, lemon juice, salt, and pepper for 1 minute. Add the oil gradually while the blender is running until mayonnaise becomes thick. Store in the refrigerator in a clean, dry container with a tight-fitting lid. Will keep for 7-10 days. **Makes approx. 350ml/12fl oz.**

# TOFU MAYONNAISE

175g/6oz soft or medium tofu
2 tablespoons lemon juice or vinegar
1/2 teaspoon salt

dash of pepper
2 tablespoons oil

In a blender or food processor, blend together (on high) the tofu, lemon juice, salt, pepper, and oil until thick and creamy. Store in the refrigerator in a clean, dry container with a tight-fitting lid. Will keep for 7-10 days. **Makes approx. 350ml/12fl oz.**

# FAUX SOUR CREAM

Since you cut sour cream out of your diet, have baked potatoes, perogies, and burritos not tasted the same? Bask again in the rapturous tang of this soy-based topping.

450g/1lb soft or medium tofu
4 tablespoons oil
3 tablespoons lemon juice or vinegar

1 teaspoon sweetener
1 tablespoon Braggs or soy sauce

In a blender or food processor, blend together all the ingredients until smooth and creamy. Store in the refrigerator in a clean, dry container with a tight-fitting lid. Will keep up to 5 days. Note: This may separate upon refrigeration and may need to be re-mixed before using.
**Makes approx. 350ml/12fl oz.**

# KLASSIC KETCHUP

After trying this sweet, savoury recipe you'll realize that shop-bought ketchup is nothing more than a pale impostor compared to the way "real" ketchup is supposed to taste.

175g/6oz tomato purée
1 1/2 tablespoons vinegar
1 tablespoon sweetener
1 teaspoon Braggs or soy sauce

1/8 teaspoon dried basil
1/8 teaspoon paprika
1/8 teaspoon salt
2 1/2 tablespoons water

In a medium saucepan, simmer all the ingredients on medium-low heat for about 10-15 minutes, stirring often. Set aside to cool and store in the refrigerator in a clean, dry container with a tight-fitting lid. This will keep for about 2 weeks, but make sure the lid is tight or it will go bad.
**Makes approx. 175ml/6fl oz.**

# CRISPY CROUTONS

Sure, lettuce and other assorted vegetables are crispy enough on their own, but your salad will shine when served up with these crunchy, toasted delights.

50g/2oz sourdough bread, cubed (pg.115)
1 tablespoon olive oil

1 teaspoon thyme
1/2 teaspoon pepper

Preheat the oven to 190°C/375°F/gas mark 5. In a large bowl, toss together all of the ingredients. Spread out evenly on a baking sheet and bake for about 10-15 minutes, until golden brown. Set aside to cool and store in a clean, dry container with a tight-fitting lid. **Makes 50g/2oz.**

# VERSATILE VEGETABLE STOCK

A flavourful stock is an important and crucial ingredient for soups and sauces. A helpful tip to ensure a delicious stock: if you won't eat what's rotting in your fridge, then don't put it into your stock. You could include vegetables that are just past their prime, or even vegetable peelings, in this recipe, but try to add at least 3 or more of the veggies listed here. Use this stock for your soups and sauces. It also freezes well.

assorted vegetables (e.g., onions, celery, carrots, potatoes, garlic), roughly chopped
2.4 litres/4 pints water
1/2 teaspoon salt
1/8 teaspoon peppercorns

Wash, cut, and prepare vegetables. Place all the ingredients into a large saucepan and bring to a boil. Turn heat down and let simmer until stock has reduced to half the original amount. Remove all the vegetables with a slotted spoon. Remove pot from heat and let the stock cool. Pour into clean, dry containers with a tight-fitting lid and store in the freezer or refrigerator. **Makes approx. 2 litres/3 1/2 pints.**

If you're not freezing the stock, use it within 5 days. If freezing, make sure you leave a little room for the stock to expand in the container.

I like to store my stock in 1 litre/1 3/4 pint containers so that if I'm going to make soup, I can pull the stock out of the freezer the night before and it will be ready for me by dinnertime. No muss, no fuss! **S**

# CAJUN SPICE

This spicy condiment sparkles up any dish that it's matched with. Use cajun spice in place of salt and pepper to season burgers, fried tofu, or tofu jerky. You can even try it to spice up your popcorn.

1 tablespoon dried onion flakes
1 teaspoon fennel seeds
1 teaspoon coriander seeds
25g/1oz chilli powder
2 teaspoons garlic powder
1 teaspoon salt
1 teaspoon dried oregano
1/4 teaspoon pepper
dash of cayenne pepper

In a blender, food processor, or coffee grinder, grind the onion flakes, fennel seeds, and coriander seeds until powdered. You can also use a rolling pin to grind the spices between 2 sheets of greaseproof paper. In a small bowl, stir together the chilli and garlic powders, salt, oregano, pepper, and cayenne pepper. Combine both mixtures and store in a clean, dry container with a tight-fitting lid. **Makes approx. 25g/1oz.**

# GOMASHIO

A simple yet wonderful Japanese condiment. Very addictive and satisfying, use it as a topping for any recipe or in place of salt on cooked vegetables or in salads or soups.

225g/8oz raw sesame seeds
1-2 teaspoons sea salt
1 teaspoon kelp powder

In a dry frying pan, heat the sesame seeds, salt, and kelp on medium-high for 3-5 minutes, stirring constantly until seeds start to pop and brown. Remove from heat and set aside to cool. Place in a blender, food processor, or coffee grinder and grind for 3 seconds. You don't want the seeds to become powdered, just lightly ground up. Store in a sealable container. **Makes 225g/8oz.**

# BALSAMIC ONIONS

This recipe can be used in a variety of ways. It's a great addition to any sauce or stir-fry, or simply delicious atop salads.

1 large onion, peeled, cut, and separated
1 teaspoon salt
$1/2$ teaspoon pepper

$11/2$ teaspoons sweetener
1 tablespoon oil
2 tablespoons balsamic vinegar

In a medium saucepan, sauté the onion, salt, pepper, and sweetener in oil on medium heat until onions are a dark golden brown, stirring often. Transfer to a medium bowl and stir onions together with the vinegar. Set aside and let sit for 10 or more minutes. **Makes 115-150g/4-5oz, depending on size of onion.**

# FAUX PARMESAN CHEESE

Simply the world's greatest faux cheese topping. Enjoy.

20g/$3/4$ oz nutritional yeast flakes
50g/2oz sesame seeds, toasted
$1/4$ teaspoon salt

In a blender, food processor, or coffee grinder, grind the yeast, sesame seeds, and salt until completely milled. Store in a clean, dry container with a tight-fitting lid. **Makes 70g/2$1/2$ oz.**

# FAUX FETA

A delightfully tangy tofu masterpiece. Use in Gourmet Greek Salad (pg. 62) or atop pizza.

4 tablespoons olive oil
4 tablespoons water
125ml/4fl oz red wine vinegar
2 teaspoons salt

1 tablespoon dried basil
1/2 teaspoon pepper
1/2 teaspoon dried oregano
225g/8oz firm herb tofu, cubed or crumbled

In a large bowl, mix together the oil, water, vinegar, salt, basil, pepper, and oregano. Marinade the tofu in the mixture for at least an hour or more. **Makes approx. 225g/8oz.**

# BAKED SESAME FRIES

Serve these yummy fries with homemade ketchup (pg. 152) or some other yummy dipping sauce. If you like to spice things up, use cajun spice (pg. 153) instead of gomashio.

4-6 large potatoes, sliced
3 tablespoons olive oil
2 tablespoons gomashio (pg. 154)

Preheat oven to 200°C/400°F/gas mark 6. Slice the potatoes to the desired width and place them in a medium bowl with some cold water. Let sit for 5 minutes. Drain potatoes and toss together with the oil and gomashio. Lay potatoes on a non-stick baking sheet and bake for 30 minutes. Flip fries after 15 minutes. **Makes 2-4 servings.**

# DRY-ROASTED SOY SNACKS

A delicious snack for any occasion.

350g/12oz dry soybeans
1-2 teaspoons seasoning (e.g., salt, cajun spice,
    pepper, red chilli flakes, cumin, curry)

In a large bowl filled with water, soak soybeans overnight. Preheat oven to 120°C/250°F/gas mark 1/2. Drain beans well and pour back into the empty large bowl. Add your desired seasoning, stirring together well, and spread out onto a large baking sheet. Bake for 3-4 hours. Let cool before serving. **Makes 450g/1lb.**

# CHICKPEA NIBBLES

A great nibbly snack.

300g/11oz cooked or canned chickpeas
1-2 teaspoons seasoning (e.g., cajun spice, pepper, red chilli flakes, cumin, garlic, curry)
1 tablespoon oil

Preheat oven to 200°C/400°F/gas mark 6. In a medium bowl, toss together the chickpeas and desired seasoning in the oil. Stir together well and spread out onto a large baking sheet. Bake for 45-60 minutes, flipping after 20 minutes. Let cool before serving. **Makes 300g/11oz.**

# ORIGINAL PEPPER TOFU JERKY

Another amazing tofu transformation. The cries of shock and pleasure should be enough to convince you that this is truly a great recipe.

450g/1lb extra-firm tofu
125ml/4fl oz Braggs or soy sauce
3-4 tablespoons liquid smoke
2 tablespoons water

1 tablespoon onion powder
1 teaspoon garlic powder or 1 clove garlic, crushed
1 tablespoon pepper
1 teaspoon sweetener

Cut the drained tofu into long narrow strips (about 5mm/1/4 in thickness). They may look big, but they will shrink during baking. In a small bowl, whisk together the Braggs, liquid smoke, water, onion powder, garlic, pepper, and sweetener. Place the tofu strips in a shallow baking tray or on a baking sheet and pour the marinade over them. Let them marinate for several hours or overnight for best results.

Cook the tofu in a food dehydrator (follow directions) or bake in the oven for about 4-6 hours at 110°C/225°F/gas mark 1/4 .

Turn the tofu over once every hour so it bakes evenly. Continue until the texture is very chewy, but not crispy. Tofu jerky will keep indefinitely. Store in a container with a tight-fitting lid.

# CAJUN JERKY

450g/1lb extra-firm tofu
125ml/4fl oz Braggs or soy sauce
3 tablespoons liquid smoke

2 tablespoons water
1 tablespoon cajun spice (pg. 153)
1 teaspoon sweetener

Cut the drained tofu into long narrow strips (about 5mm/1/4 in thickness). They may look big, but they will shrink during baking. In a small bowl, whisk together the Braggs, liquid smoke, water, cajun spice, and sweetener. Place the tofu strips in a shallow baking tray or baking sheet and pour the marinade over them. Let them marinate for several hours or overnight for best results.

Cook the tofu in a food dehydrator (follow directions) or bake in the oven for about 4-6 hours at 110°C/225°F/gas mark 1/2.

Turn the tofu over once every hour so it bakes evenly. Continue until the texture is very chewy, but not crispy. Tofu jerky will keep indefinitely. Store in a container with a tight-fitting lid.

# HAWAIIAN JERKY

450g/1lb extra-firm tofu
2 tablespoons Braggs or soy sauce
125ml/4fl oz pineapple juice
1 teaspoon ground ginger

1/4 teaspoon pepper
1/8 teaspoon cayenne pepper
1 teaspoon garlic powder
1 tablespoon sweetener

Cut the drained tofu into long narrow strips (about 5mm/1/4 in thickness). They may look big, but they will shrink during baking. In a small bowl, whisk together the Braggs, pineapple juice, ginger, pepper, cayenne pepper, garlic powder, and sweetener. Place the tofu strips in a shallow baking tray or on a baking sheet and pour the marinade over them. Let them marinate for several hours or overnight for best results.

Cook the tofu in a food dehydrator (follow directions) or bake in the oven for about 4-6 hours at 110°C/225°F/gas mark 1/2.

Turn the tofu over once every hour so it bakes evenly. Continue until the texture is very chewy, but not crispy. Tofu jerky will keep indefinitely. Store in a container with a tight-fitting lid.

# VEGAN KIDS STUFF

Some of my fondest childhood memories come from the kitchen. The smells, sounds, and tastes that surrounded me as a child helped me to become the vegan food-lover I am today. I remember sitting on the kitchen table in an apron that covered my feet, food all over my hands and face, helping to pour ingredients into my Mum's big beige mixing bowl. I felt terribly important and was proud to help. S

Children love to lend a hand in the kitchen. We're all busy trying to do too much in too little time; when it comes to food, we grab a quick bite, order in, or make something that requires only water and a microwave. But that's not really eating. We need to take the time to slow down and teach ourselves and our children to savour the food we eat, to appreciate what we put into our bodies.

In this chapter we have included recipes that the children in your life can help with and some they can do on their own, as well as activities to keep them busy. We've also included tried and true, yummy recipes to please even the pickiest eater.

Our wish is that you pass on an appreciation for healthy food and spend some time with your kids in the kitchen making memories to last a lifetime.

# TIPS FOR FEEDING KIDS

## Eat together

We're all busy. Do you occasionally find yourself eating in front of the TV or standing over the hob picking out of a pan? We grab meals when we can. But the single most important thing you can do to give your kids healthy attitudes toward food is to sit down at the table and eat with them. It's also important to eat what they're eating instead of serving separate "grown-up food" and "kid food". Talk about your meal, how it tastes and smells. Create eating experiences that are significant, happy times that involve conversation and laughter as well as nourishment. Above all, keep your meal free of stressful nagging and criticism.

## Monkey see, monkey do

While considering your child's eating habits, take a good look at your own. Children learn from your example, so you owe it to them, and to yourself, to improve your own eating habits.

- Eat a good, hearty breakfast. A full belly makes for a happy and attentive child.

- Eat your veggies! Let your children see you eating and enjoying raw vegetables.

- Eat healthy snacks. Instead of junk food, nibble on fresh and dried fruit, vegetable sticks, soy yoghurt, and air-popped popcorn. Check pgs. 165-169 for some good snack ideas.

## Offer healthy foods

Children won't crave or beg for biscuits and sweets if they are never around or offered. Keep around only the foods you want your kids to eat. Have fresh fruit, celery and carrot sticks, radishes, cucumbers, and other vegetables washed, cut, and available in the fridge. In the summer, try juice lollies (pg. 173) or tofudge lollies (pg. 172).

## Don't forbid any foods

This may sound like a contradiction, but it's best not to make a big deal out of "bad" foods. Even though we wish our kids never touched junk food, let them have it once in a while. By allowing kids to eat what they want at birthday parties and school outings, they'll learn that junk food is something to be eaten sporadically. They'll also learn the important lesson that these foods can occasionally fit into an overall healthy diet.

## How much to eat

Many parents agonize over how little or how much their children consume. Children whose parents aren't overly controlling of their food intake are in a better position to regulate how much they eat themselves. Remember that your child is much smaller than you and requires smaller portions. He or she also needs to eat more frequently. A good rule for children under six is to serve one tablespoon of each food item for each year at each meal. For example, serve three tablespoons of apple sauce to a three-year-old. Kids' food intake will vary as their growth speeds up and slows down. Some days they may seem to eat very little, but they will make up for it by eating more the next day or the day after. By letting kids decide when to have more and when they've had enough, you are helping them to recognize the internal cues of hunger and fullness. These cues will help them regulate their food intake and weight for life.

Limit fruit juice intake to 125ml/4fl oz per day. Offer juice after meals, and not before when it may curb a child's appetite for more wholesome foods. Some children may better tolerate white grape juice than apple juice. Offer fresh filtered water at all times. Clean, clear water is the best way to a healthy body.

## What to eat

Encourage your child to help plan meals and select veggies at the market. Get them involved in meal preparation. Even a two-year-old can tear lettuce for a salad and help wash produce. You can ease tensions at the table by including them in decisions on what to make for dinner. Children will take pride in a meal they've helped to plan and prepare. Encourage your children to try everything you offer, but don't force them to eat what they don't want. Don't make a fuss if they refuse a certain dish. Eventually they'll come around. We've heard too many horror stories about parents who force their kids to eat foods they don't want. Food is not about power; it's about nourishment. If your child is picky, take a deep breath and be patient.

## Don't use food as a weapon

Never use food as a bribe or a reward. And never send kids to bed without supper, or keep them at the table until they've cleared their plates. Let food be what it is – a source of nourishment and enjoyment.

## Teach them to love vegetables

Some vegetables have strong flavours and many kids will refuse to try them. Introduce a variety of different vegetables into your child's diet as soon as possible. They'll quickly become accustomed to the tastes. Don't force anything on your child; just offer and encourage. Always keep fruits and vegetables in the fridge, washed, cut, and ready to eat. Remember that calories, not protein, are the main issue with young children. While it's important to have raw fruits and vegetables in any child's diet, don't forget about high-density foods such as tofu, nut and seed butters, avocados, and olives.

Let kids grow their own food. They will be fascinated by the process of seeds turning into plants. Even if you only have a flowerpot on the kitchen window sill, it's easy to grow vegetables such as beansprouts, parsley, and radishes.

## Raising healthy eaters

Ours is an obsessed, sick, and sad culture! Children, especially girls, as young as nine and even younger are dieting and worrying about their figures. It has got to stop. You can help by teaching your children to love their bodies, their imaginations, and the food they eat. It all starts in the kitchen.

# FUN IN THE KITCHEN

Have you ever noticed that kids are at their most difficult just as you're working on making that perfect vegan cream sauce? Here are some ideas to keep them busy and out of your hair while you're cooking meals:

## Doing Their Own Thing

Get a plastic storage container and fill it with items such as a kids-sized apron, plastic utensils, wooden spoons, small bowls, measuring spoons, empty spice jars, and a small rolling pin. Let them pretend they're making dinner when you are. Or allow them to help when you're baking or cooking, using their own kitchen utensils.

## Edible Necklace

This is a good project to bring along before heading to the supermarket with your kids. They can munch on the necklace while shopping. Get some healthy cereal and/or sweets with holes, as well as some healthy shoestring liquorice. Have your kids thread the sweets or cereal on the liquorice. When complete, tie the ends together. This will keep them busy noshing while you do other things!

## Flour Fun

Sprinkle flour over a baking sheet. They can draw letters, numbers, shapes. Play hangman or other common games in the flour.

## Painting with Pudding

This makes clean-up a lot of fun because it's lickable! Prepare the pudding recipe on page 146 ahead of time. When it's ready, let your kids fingerpaint with the pudding on greaseproof paper (or a clean table, if you dare!).

## Personal Place Mats

Personal place mats make eating special. They also make excellent gifts! Get some heavy paper or card, crayons, glue, glitter and anything else you can think of. Let the kids draw their own pictures on the paper, adding whatever other elements they have. Use clear sticky-back plastic to cover the front and back of the drawing or have it laminated.

## Pasta Pictures and Sculptures

Use various shapes of pasta for different looks. Let your kids glue these onto coloured paper for imaginative 3-D pictures.

## Taste Testing

Clean and cut up various food items. Blindfold your child and have them taste and smell different foods. Get them to describe the various tastes, smells, and textures before they try to guess what it is. For fun, tell them that olives are eyeballs and cooked spaghetti are brains and watch the looks on their faces!

## PLAY DOUGH

Every kid deserves to play with play dough, especially if it's home-made.

115g/4oz flour
salt
2 tablespoons oil

2 tablespoons cream of tartar
250ml/8fl oz water
food colouring

In a medium saucepan, cook the flour, salt, oil, tartar, and water over medium-high heat, stirring constantly until stiff. Cool and knead out lumps while kneading in the food colouring. Store in a container with a tight-fitting lid.

## ORNAMENTS

115g/4oz cornflour
225g/8oz bicarbonate of soda
300ml/1/2 pint cold water

In a medium saucepan, cook the cornflour, bicarbonate of soda, and water over medium-high heat, stirring constantly, for about 4 minutes or until mixture thickens into a moist, mashed potato-like consistency. Place in a bowl and cover with a cloth until its cool enough to knead. Knead well and roll out the dough to cut into shapes. Use a straw to place a small hole in the top for a ribbon or string so you can hang the ornament somewhere special. Allow to dry for 24 hours before painting.

You can also use this recipe for making sculptures. Form clay into desired shapes and let dry for 36 hours before painting.

## GLUE

Use a paintbrush, lolly stick, or even your fingers to spread this glue!

50g/2oz flour
125ml/4fl oz water
1 tablespoon salt

In a small bowl, mix the flour, water and salt together. Stir until paste is creamy. You can store left-over glue in a clean, dry jar with a tight-fitting lid. **Makes approximately 250ml/8fl oz.**

# PAPIER-MÂCHÉ

115g/4oz flour
2 tablespoons salt (prevents moulding)
250ml/8fl oz water
newspaper strips

In a large bowl, mix the flour, salt, and water together until smooth. Cut newspaper into strips and soak them in the mixture. Use your fingers to squeeze off excess paste and layer on to whatever base you are using (balloon, wire rim, etc.). Allow to dry for 24 hours before painting.

# BUBBLE SOLUTION

You can make your own bubble wands by twisting one end of a pipe cleaner into a large loop, or use a straw as a bubble pipe.

175ml/6fl oz liquid soap
250ml/8fl oz water
4 tablespoons golden syrup or light runny honey

Place soap, water, and golden syrup in a clean, dry jar. Stir together with a large spoon.
**Makes approximately 475ml/16fl oz of solution.**

# FUN SNACKS FOR KIDS

Let your children have some control over when and how much they eat. Even toddlers can have their own personal snack shelf stocked with bread sticks, dried fruit, and other nutritious snacks. Snacking is an important way for young children to get the calories they need. Spend some time getting messy, and exploring different taste combinations. Your kids will love to make these recipes with you!

## MELON BOWL

watermelon
various other melons
melon baller or spoon

Cut a watermelon in half. If your kids are old enough, have them help scoop out the inside using a small spoon or melon baller. Set aside in a separate bowl. Cut the other melons and have the kids scoop them out, then fill the watermelon bowl with the various melon balls. Serve with fruit sauce (pg. 146) or apple dip (pg.167).

## ANTS ON A LOG

Munch away on these little ants.

celery sticks, washed
peanut butter or nut butter
raisins

If your kids are old enough, let them use a dull knife to fill up the centre cavity of the celery sticks with the nut butter. Top with raisins.

## ANTS ON A RAFT

crackers
peanut butter or nut butter
raisins

If your kids are old enough, let them use a blunt knife to spread the nut butter on the crackers. Top with raisins. If you like, you can use jam or some other spread for your creations.

# DROWNING ANTS

bowl of soy yoghurt or pudding (pgs. 146-147)
raisins

Mix the raisins in the bowl of yoghurt or pudding. Get your kids to try to fish out the ants and eat them!

# APPLE VOLCANO

apple, top removed
peanut butter or nut spread
raisins

Using a teaspoon, help your child scoop out the inside of the apple. Fill it with peanut butter and top with raisins. If this is to be eaten later, brush apple edges with lemon juice to prevent browning and wrap in foil.

# BANANA CREAM PIE

Super messy but that's what being in the kitchen is all about!

banana
digestive biscuits
whipped cream (pg. 145)

Have your kids tear up the banana into bite-size pieces. Place on digestive biscuits, then add a glob of whipped cream. Place another digestive biscuit on top and then squish it down.

# ICE CREAM BISCUITS

biscuits
ice cream (pgs. 148-149) or whipped cream (pg. 145)

Spread 1/2 teaspoon of ice cream or whipped cream between 2 biscuits. Freeze for 30-60 minutes.

# MAPLE APPLE DIP

A great after-school snack.

225g/8oz silken tofu
1/2 teaspoon cinnamon
1/2 teaspoon vanilla extract

4 tablespoons apple syrup
1-2 medium apples, sliced

In a blender or food processor, blend together the tofu, cinnamon, vanilla, and maple syrup until smooth. Spoon into a small bowl and use as a dip for the slices of apple and other fruits. **Makes approximately 350ml/12fl oz.**

# HUKI-LA SMOOTHIE

This recipe is also great frozen. Pour into lolly moulds and eat on a hot summer day.

2-4 ice cubes
225g/8oz silken or soft tofu
4-6 strawberries
250ml/8fl oz guava or tropical fruit juice

1 banana, frozen
120ml/4fl oz pineapple or apple juice
25g/1oz pineapple (optional)

In a blender or food processor, blend together all the ingredients until creamy. Garnish with more pineapple. **Makes 2 servings.**

# FRESH FRUIT KEBABS

wooden skewers (1 per person)
bananas, chopped
eating apples, chopped
green, red, and purple grapes

pineapple chunks
melon, chopped
apple dip ( above) or soy yoghurt
desiccated coconut

Cut the fruit into bite-sized chunks. Pour dip onto a large plate, and the desiccated coconut onto another plate. Slide pieces of fruit onto each skewer, making sure to include a piece of each kind of fruit, and leaving enough room for your fingers to grab. Hold the kebab at each end and roll it in the dip, and then in the coconut.

If you like, you can roll the kebabs in something other than coconut; try muesli, nuts, or raisins.

# TRAVELLERS' TRAIL MIX

When you're hungry for a snack, reach in and munch away.

muesli (pg. 45)
nuts and seeds (e.g., peanuts, cashews, almonds,
    sunflower seeds)

dried fruit (e.g., raisins, apricots, cranberries)
cereal rings
carob chips

Add all the ingredients in a small plastic bag or clean, dry jar. Seal it tight and then shake until well-mixed.


# VEGGIES IN A BLANKET

You can add any veggies you want to this recipe. The more the merrier!

2 flour tortillas
2 tablespoons cream cheese (pg. 81)

1 carrot, grated
2 lettuce leaves

Warm the tortillas in a dry pan on low heat. Lay each one on a plate and lightly spread the cream cheese over each. Add carrots and lettuce (or whatever vegetables you choose), and roll. **Makes    2 servings.**


# EDIBLE VEGGIE BOWL

A portable, totally edible veggie treat. After you've eaten the veggies, you can eat the bowl!

green, yellow, or red pepper, cored
celery, chopped
carrots, chopped

broccoli, chopped
mangetout, chopped
creamy salad dressing (pgs. 69-73)

Cut the pepper in half width-wise. Remove the seeds and the white veins from the inside. Now you have two pieces, one of which will be your bowl. Cut the other half of the pepper into thin slices. Cut the celery, carrots, broccoli, and mangetout into bite-size pieces and add to the pepper slices. Spoon a little salad dressing into the bottom of your pepper bowl and place the assorted veggies inside.

# MEALS FOR THE PICKY

When it comes to making meals for kids, let go of any rigid ideas you may have about what goes into a meal and experiment with ingredients to come up with recipes they will love. Even better, let them in on the process and help with making the meal! These recipes have been tested on some of the pickiest eaters out there. Let's hope they work on yours.

## ALPHABET LENTILS

ABCDEFG, eat your lentils 1-2-3!

175g/6oz dry lentils
1 small onion, finely chopped
1 carrot, finely diced
4 mushrooms, finely chopped

250ml/8fl oz tomato sauce (pgs.76-77)
600ml/1 pint vegetable stock
2 tablespoons Braggs or soy sauce
50g/2oz dry alphabet pasta

In a medium saucepan, combine the lentils, onion, carrot, mushrooms, tomato sauce, stock, and Braggs. Cover and simmer for 20-30 minutes, or until lentils are tender. Add the dry pasta. Cover and simmer for 10 more minutes, or until the pasta is tender, stirring occasionally. **Makes 2 servings.**

## NUTTY BROCCOLI

Serve this and watch with amazement as they gobble it up.

2 tablespoons peanut butter or nut butter
1 tablespoon Braggs or soy sauce
1 tablespoon orange or apple juice
115g/4oz broccoli, chopped

In a small saucepan on medium heat, stir together the nut butter, Braggs, and orange juice. Heat until warmed through. Meanwhile, steam broccoli for about 3 minutes until it is tender but not fragile. Drain and toss with the sauce. **Makes 1-2 servings.**

# NUTTY HUMMUS DIP

Serve with an assortment of vegetables sticks, fruit slices, and crackers.

90g/3½ oz cooked or canned chickpeas
4 tablespoons peanut butter or nut butter
4 tablespoons apple juice

½ teaspoon cinnamon
4 tablespoons any jam or fruit spread

In a blender or food processor, blend together the chickpeas, nut butter, apple juice, and cinnamon until smooth. Spoon into a medium serving bowl, and top with a layer of jam or fruit spread. **Makes 2-4 servings.**

# CARROT RAISIN SAUCE

You can heat this sauce up if need be, or just stir into warm rice and serve.

125g/4oz carrot, grated
4 tablespoons water
50g/2oz soft tofu
2 teaspoons Braggs or soy sauce

1 teaspoon toasted sesame oil
⅛ teaspoon fresh ginger, grated
raisins (garnish)

In a blender or food processor, blend together the carrots, water, tofu, Braggs, sesame oil, and ginger. Garnish with raisins. **Makes 1 serving.**

# ORANGE RAISIN SAUCE

You can also heat up this sauce or add to warm rice or pasta.

90g/3½ oz cooked or canned chickpeas
1 teaspoon Braggs or soy sauce
4-5 tablespoons orange juice

½ teaspoon mild curry powder
40g/1½ oz raisins

In a blender or food processor, blend together the chickpeas, Braggs, orange juice, and curry until smooth. Stir in the raisins. You may add peas, carrots, or any other vegetables. **Makes 1 serving.**

# FART SANDWICH

The best part about being a vegan kid is the vegan farts!

40g/1½ oz re-fried black beans (pg. 93)
2 slices of bread
cucumber slices

mild salsa (pg. 86)
soy cheese (optional)

Spread the beans on a slice of bread. Add the cucumbers, salsa, and cheese on top. Cover with other slice of bread.

# FART ROLL

You can add salsa to this if your kids are feeling spicy!

25-40g/1-1 1/2 oz re-fried black beans (pg. 93)
tortilla shell
tomatoes, sliced
cucumbers, sliced
lettuce, shredded
beansprouts

Spread the beans on the tortilla. Add the tomato, cucumber, lettuce, and beansprouts in a thin layer on top, then roll up the tortilla.

# QUICKIE FAUX EGG SALAD SANDWICH

Check out our other faux egg salad on pg. 64.

115g/4oz medium or firm tofu
2-3 tablespoons soy mayonnaise (pg.151)
1/4 teaspoon turmeric
1 tablespoon celery, finely diced
1 teaspoon red or green onion, finely diced
dash of pepper
4 slices of bread
1/4 teaspoon Dijon mustard (optional)

In a small bowl, mash together the tofu, mayonnaise, and turmeric. Stir in the celery, onions, pepper, and optional mustard. Spread between slices of bread. You can add beansprouts, lettuce, grated carrots, or anything else that tickles your fancy.

# ELVIS FRIED SANDWICH

Thank you. Thank you very much.

margarine
2 slices of bread
peanut butter or nut butter
1/2 banana, thinly sliced

Spread a thin layer of margarine on both slices of bread. On the other side of one slice, spread a layer of nut butter (beware: this gets a little messy). Lay the slice margarine-side down in a frying pan and add banana slices, and top with the other slice of bread, margarine-side up. Fry until golden, flip, and once done, serve. Dip in maple syrup if you like!

# RABBIT SHAKE

Hup-sha, hup-sha, quick like a bunny.

115g/4oz soft or silken tofu
250-475ml/8-16fl oz orange or apple juice
1 banana (frozen works best)
1 carrot, finely grated

Combine all ingredients in a blender, and blend on high speed until very smooth.
**Makes 1-2 servings.**


# TOFUDGE LOLLIES

A sweet, cool treat.

225g/8oz soft or silken tofu
120ml/4fl oz soy milk
65g/2 1/2 oz sweetener
25g/1oz carob or cocoa powder
2 teaspoons vanilla extract

1/4 teaspoon cinnamon
1 teaspoon Inka grain beverage (optional)
dash of salt
lolly moulds

In a blender or food processor, blend together all the ingredients until very smooth and creamy.
Pour into lolly moulds and freeze. Remove from freezer 5 minutes before serving. **Makes 8-12,
depending on moulds.**


# ORANGE LOLLIES

50g/2oz soft or silken tofu
250ml/8fl oz soy milk
175ml/6fl oz frozen orange juice concentrate

50g/2oz sweetener
1 teaspoon vanilla extract
lolly moulds

In a blender or food processor, blend together all the ingredients until very smooth and creamy.
Pour into lolly moulds and freeze. Remove from freezer 5 minutes before serving. **Makes 8-12,
depending on moulds.**

## SMOOTHIE ICE POPS

The coolest summer dessert you can find.

115g/4oz fruit (e.g., strawberries, blueberries)
1 banana, chopped
225g/8oz soft tofu
120ml/4fl oz soy milk

120ml/4fl oz fruit juice (e.g., pineapple, apple, guava)
lolly moulds

In a blender or food processor, blend together all the ingredients until very smooth and creamy. Pour into lolly moulds and freeze. Remove from freezer 5 minutes before serving. **Makes 8-12, depending on moulds.**

## JUICE LOLLIES

Sugar-free and simple to make. My mum used to let me make different combinations, like: grape/apple or orange/papaya. Let them decide! **S**

various juices
lolly moulds

Pour juice into lolly moulds and freeze. Remove from freezer 5 minutes before serving.

# FEEDING KIDS ON THE ROAD

There's a simple rule of the road: feed children when they're hungry. Full tummies make for happier travellers. At rest stops, buy juice and oatcakes rather than cola drinks, sweets, or crisps. Avoid salty snacks and sugary drinks. Remember to offer LOTS of water. There may be more pee stops, but it's important to keep hydrated!

## Foods to Pack for an Outing or Trip

- dried apricots, figs, prunes, cranberries
- small juice boxes or cans of juice
- small soy milk boxes
- small cans of vegetable juice
- jars of natural baby food
- wheatgerm or oat bran (add it to cold or hot cereal, on salads, in soups)
- trail mix (pg. 168)
- tofu jerky (pgs. 156-157)
- bottled water

# VEGAN HOUSE & HOME

Today's market is saturated with house-cleaning and beauty products. Our ancestors lived for hundreds of years without these kinds of products; their houses looked great, and so did they! Most shop-bought products do tremendous amounts of damage to our environment, not to mention all the waste due to over-packaging. Some companies offer goods that are "green" and/or animal cruelty-free, but you still have to deal with all that packaging. With the recipes and ideas offered in this chapter, you can look great and live in a clean and safe home environment without harming the planet.

# HOUSEHOLD CLEANERS

If you're looking for alternatives to standard household cleaning products, try some of the following formulas and techniques. They are safer for your home, your children, your animal friends, and the environment. And they cost less!

### All-Purpose Cleaner
- Mix vinegar and salt for a good surface cleaner.
- Pour some bicarbonate of soda and vinegar on a damp sponge. It will clean and deodorise all kitchen and bathroom surfaces.

### Deodoriser
- Place partially filled saucers of vinegar around the room.
- Boil 1 tablespoon of vinegar in 250ml/8fl oz of water to eliminate unpleasant cooking odours.
- Bicarbonate of soda is excellent for absorbing odours.

### Removing crayon marks
- Crayon marks on the floor or table can be removed by rubbing them with some toothpaste on a damp cloth. Don't use this on wallpaper or porous surfaces.

### Removing grease spots
- Immediately pour salt on grease spots to absorb and prevent staining.

### Removing scratches
- Mix equal parts of lemon juice and vegetable oil, and rub against scratches with a soft cloth until they disappear.

### Laundry starch
- Dissolve 1 tablespoon of cornflour in 475ml/16fl oz of cold water. Place in a spray bottle. Shake well before using. Make sure to label this so you don't use it for cleaning.

### Oven cleaner
- While the oven is still warm, pour some salt on grimy areas. If the areas are dry, dampen with water before applying the salt. When the oven cools down, scrape the grime off and wash clean.

# 45 THINGS TO DO WITH VINEGAR

1. Kill weeds. Spray full-strength on growth until weeds have starved.

2. Kill unwanted grass on walks and driveways.

3. Increase soil acidity. Use 120ml/4fl oz of vinegar in 3.75 litres/6½ pints tap water for watering plants such as rhododendrons, gardenias, or azaleas.

4. Deter ants. Spray vinegar around doors, appliances, and along other areas where ants are.

5. Polish car chrome. Apply full-strength.

6. Remove odours from a dog. Rub fur with full-strength vinegar and rinse.

7. Keep cats away. Sprinkle vinegar on areas you don't want the cat walking, sleeping, or scratching.

8. Keep dogs from scratching their ears. Use a clean, soft cloth dipped in vinegar diluted with water.

9. Floor cleaner. Mix 250ml/8fl oz white vinegar with 7.5 litres/12 pints hot water.

10. Freshen wilted vegetables. Soak them in 475ml/16fl oz of water and a tablespoon of vinegar.

11. Soothe a bee or jellyfish sting. Dot the irritation with vinegar to relieve itching.

12. Relieve sunburn. Lightly rub on white vinegar. You may have to reapply.

13. Condition hair. Add a tablespoon of vinegar to dissolve sticky residue left by shampoo.

14. Relieve dry and itchy skin. Add 2 tablespoons to bath water.

15. Fight dandruff. See page 182 for recipe.

16. Soothe a sore throat. Pour a teaspoon of cider vinegar in a glass of water. Gargle, then swallow.

17. Treat sinus infections and chest colds. Add 4 tablespoons or more of vinegar to a vaporiser.

19. Deodorise the kitchen drain. Pour 250ml/8fl oz down the drain once a week. Let stand 30 minutes and then flush with cold water.

20. Eliminate onion odours. Rub on your fingers before and after slicing.

21. Clean and disinfect wood cutting boards. Wipe with full-strength vinegar.

22. Remove fruit stains from hands. Rub with vinegar.

23. Cut grease and odour on dishes. Add a tablespoon of vinegar to hot soapy water.

24. Clean a teapot. Boil a mixture of water and vinegar in the teapot. Wipe away the grime.

25. Freshen a lunchbox. Soak a piece of bread in vinegar and let it sit in the lunchbox overnight.

26. Clean the refrigerator. Wash with a solution of equal parts water and vinegar.

27. Unclog a drain. Pour a handful of bicarbonate of soda down the drain, add 120ml/4fl oz vinegar, and close with plug for 20 seconds. Rinse with hot water.

28. Clean and deodorise jars. Rinse mayonnaise, peanut butter, and mustard jars with vinegar when empty.

29. Clean the dishwasher. Run 250ml/8fl oz of vinegar through the whole cycle once a month to reduce soap build-up on the inner mechanisms and on glassware.

30. Clean stainless steel. Wipe with a vinegar-dampened cloth.

31. Remove stains from pans. Fill the pan with a solution of 3 tablespoons of vinegar to 600ml/1 pint of water. Boil until stain loosens and can be washed away.

32. Clean the microwave. Boil a solution of 4 tablespoons vinegar and 250ml/8fl oz of water in the microwave. Will loosen food particles from microwave walls and deodorise.

33. Dissolve rust from bolts and other metals. Soak in full-strength vinegar.

34. Eliminate cooking smells. Let simmer a small pot of vinegar and water solution.

35. Unclog steam iron. Pour equal amounts of vinegar and water into the iron's water chamber. Turn to steam and leave the iron on for 5 minutes in an upright position. Then unplug and allow to cool. Any loose particles should come out when you empty the water.

36. Clean a scorched iron plate. Heat equal parts vinegar and salt in a small pan. Rub solution on the cooled iron surface to remove dark or burned stains.

37. Remove lint from clothes. Add 120m/4fl oz of vinegar to the rinse cycle of the washing machine. This also helps to brighten fabric colours.

38. Freshen the washing machine. Pour 250ml/8fl oz of vinegar in the machine and let it run through a regular cycle (no clothes added). Will dissolve soap residue.

39. Remove tough stains. Gently rub vinegar on the stains before placing in the washing machine.

40. Eliminate smoke odours from clothes. Add 250ml/8fl oz of vinegar to a bathtub of hot water. Hang clothes above the steam.

41. Remove transfers. Brush with a couple of coats of vinegar and allow to soak in before washing off.

42. Clean eyeglasses. Wipe each lens with a drop of vinegar.

43. Freshen cut flowers. Add 2 tablespoons of vinegar and 1 teaspoon of sugar for 1 litre/1³/4 pints of water.

44. Extinguish fires. Throw on grease fires to arrest flames.

45. Feel good. A teaspoon of cider vinegar in a glass of water, with a bit of sweetener added for flavour, will give you an overall healthy feeling.

# HEALTH & BEAUTY PRODUCTS

Here are a few beauty products you can make in your own kitchen. It will save you some money, save the animals, and save your skin! Remember: these recipes have no preservatives, so the recipes are for small amounts. Use them up quickly and ALWAYS label your bottles so there won't be any accidents! Also, be sure to test a small area for skin sensitivity before using any mixture. Dab a little on the inside of your wrist or underside of your arm and let sit for 30-40 minutes. Wait 24-48 hours and see if it causes a reaction such as a rash. If not, you're free to use it.

## MAKEUP REMOVER

Apply vegetable oil, shortening, or vitamin E oil to skin and tissue off. This is a simple and effective makeup remover.

## NORMAL SKIN CLEANSER

2 tablespoons lemon juice

6 tablespoons vegetable shortening

In a blender or food processor, blend together the lemon juice and vegetable shortening until well mixed. Apply to your face and tissue off. Store in the refrigerator in a clean, dry jar with a tight-fitting lid.

## FRUITY FACE CLEANSER

For oily or combination skin. Tomatoes are highly acidic, so be careful using this cleanser if you have sensitive skin.

50g/2oz apple
50g/2oz cucumber

50g/2oz tomatoes or peaches

In a blender or food processor, blend together the apple, cucumber, and tomatoes or peaches. Store in the refrigerator in a clean, dry jar with a tight-fitting lid. Use 1 teaspoon as a cleanser. Apply to face, wait 15-30 seconds, and rinse with warm water.

## PARSLEY SKIN TONER

For normal or dry skin. Parsley is a wonderful skin softener and toner.

25g/1oz fresh parsley, chopped

250ml/8fl oz boiling water

In a medium bowl, place the chopped parsley and cover with boiling water. Allow to cool completely. Strain and pour into a clean jar with a tight-fitting lid. Apply to skin with a cotton ball.

# LEMON TONER

For oily or combination skin. Witch hazel is a natural, non-drying astringent distilled from the witch hazel shrub.

125ml/4fl oz lemon juice
250ml/8fl oz water
100ml/3 1/2fl oz witch hazel

In a clean, dry jar, combine the lemon juice, water, and witch hazel. Cap tightly and shake well before using. Apply with a cotton ball.

# GREEN GODDESS MASK

For dry skin.

1 avocado

In a blender, food processor, or with a fork, blend together the flesh of the avocado into a creamy texture. Massage into your face and neck. Tissue off after 10-15 minutes with warm water and then apply a toner.

# HOT MEDITERRANEAN MOMMA MASK

For normal skin.

40g/1 1/2 oz mashed, cooked or canned chickpeas
1 tablespoon olive or flax oil
1/4 teaspoon lemon juice

In a blender or food processor, or with a fork, blend all ingredients into a creamy texture. Apply mixture to your face and leave on for 15-20 minutes. Rinse with warm, then cool, water.

# CUCUMBER LEMON MASK

For oily skin.

1/2 cucumber, chopped
1 tablespoon lemon juice
1 teaspoon fresh mint

In a blender or food processor, blend together the cucumber, lemon juice, and mint until well-mixed. Refrigerate for 10 minutes. Apply mixture to your face and leave on for 10-15 minutes. Rinse with warm, then cool, water.

# BLEMISHED SKIN MASK

Again, note that tomatoes are highly acidic so be careful using this cleanser if you have sensitive skin.

1 tomato, finely chopped
1 teaspoon lemon juice

1 tablespoon cooked oatmeal

In a blender or food processor, blend together the tomato, lemon juice, and oatmeal until well-mixed. Apply mixture to your face, making sure it is thick enough to stay on blemished areas: cheeks, forehead, or chin. Leave on for 5-10 minutes, then scrub off with a clean flannel dipped in warm water.

# OATMEAL ALMOND FACIAL SCRUB

4 tablespoons rolled oat flakes
25g/1oz almonds

water

In a food processor, grind the oat flakes and almonds to a fine consistency. Slowly add water until it becomes a paste. Apply mixture to your face and massage. Rinse with cool water.

# PIMPLE KILLER

Garlic clears out your pores, acting as a remedy for pimples. Peel and mash a garlic clove. Apply the paste to your pimple (being careful to avoid contact with your eyes) and leave on for 15 minutes. Wash off with a warm cloth. Warning: this can be very smelly, and even more so as it rinses off.

# POTATO EYE REMEDY

This recipe will lighten dark circles under your eyes and tighten your skin. Wrap a grated raw potato in muslin and apply to closed eyelids for 15-20 minutes. Wipe off residue with a cloth rinsed in cool water and apply an eye cream.

# DIRTY BOY SHAMPOO

For really dirty hair!

175ml/6fl oz warm water
120ml/4fl oz animal-friendly shampoo
1½ teaspoons salt

2 teaspoons jojoba oil
1/8 teaspoon peppermint essential oil

In a clean, dry container add the water, shampoo, salt, jojoba oil, and peppermint oil. Cap tightly and shake until well-blended.

# QUICK CIDER VINEGAR CONDITIONER

A weak vinegar rinse is the best conditioner you can use after shampooing. It restores the natural acid balance to the hair and takes out any traces of soap and grime.

1 tablespoon cider vinegar
1 litre/13/4 pints water

Place vinegar and water in a clean, dry container and cap tightly. Shake well. After shampooing, work through and rinse. Use 250-475ml/8-16fl oz depending on hair length.

# SAGE RINSE

475ml/16fl oz red wine vinegar
475ml/16fl oz water
4 tablespoons fresh sage

Combine vinegar, water, and sage in medium saucepan. Bring to a boil and reduce heat to low. Simmer uncovered for 15 minutes, then cover pot, remove from heat, and let steep for 30 minutes. Strain out sage, and once the rinse has cooled, store in a clean, dry container with a tight-fitting lid. After shampooing, pour 120ml/4fl oz over your hair, then rinse.

# RINSE FOR DAMAGED HAIR

4 tablespoons  kelp powder
250ml/8fl oz Sage Rinse mixture (see above)

Combine kelp and Sage Rinse in a clean, dry container. Cap tightly and shake well. Apply generously to freshly shampooed hair. Leave on for 20 minutes, then rinse thoroughly.

# HOT OIL TREATMENT FOR DRY HAIR

Not for fine hair.

4 tablespoons olive oil
4 tablespoons very hot water

Place olive oil and hot water in a clean, dry container, cap tightly, and shake very well. Massage into dry hair. Put a shower cap or plastic bag over your hair and wrap your head in a towel. Leave mixture on your hair for 15-20 minutes. This is important: when you are ready to rinse, apply shampoo directly to your hair without washing out the oil treatment. Then rinse, apply shampoo again, and condition as usual. (If you apply water before you apply shampoo, you'll have a hard time getting the oil out.)

# DANDRUFF TREATMENT

2 tablespoons cider vinegar
2 tablespoons water
2 tablespoons flax oil or olive oil

In a clean, dry container, combine the vinegar, water, and oil. Cap tightly and shake until well mixed. Massage into your scalp and leave on for 15-20 minutes. Shampoo out.

# CINNAMON TOOTHPASTE

Forget your toothpaste at home? This spicy toothpaste will help keep your teeth pearly white and your breath fresh. Bicarbonate of soda neutralises acids from plaque, helping to prevent gingivitis or gum disease.

1 teaspoon bicarbonate of soda
1/4 teaspoon cinnamon
1 drop tea tree essential oil (optional)

In a cup or small bowl, mix together the soda, cinnamon, and tea tree oil. Place damp toothbrush into the mixture and brush teeth.

# PEPPERMINT-CLOVE TOOTHPASTE

1/2 teaspoon bicarbonate of soda
1/2 teaspoon sea salt
1 drop clove essential oil
1 drop peppermint essential oil

In a cup or small bowl, mix together the soda, salt, and oils. Place damp toothbrush into mixture and brush teeth.

# TEA TREE-PEPPERMINT MOUTHWASH

300ml/1/2 pint water
6 drops tea tree essential oil
6 drops peppermint essential oil

Pour water and oils into a clean, dry container. Cap tightly and shake well. Rinse mouth out, but do not swallow.

# HERBAL MOUTHWASH

2 tablespoons fresh rosemary, parsley, or mint
2 whole cloves
475ml/16fl oz water

In a small saucepan, bring water and chosen herb to a boil. Reduce heat and simmer for 15-20 minutes. Set aside to cool. Strain into a clean, dry jar and cap tightly. Rinse mouth out, but do not swallow.

# BATH SALTS

115g/4oz sea salt
115g/4oz bicarbonate of soda
175g/6oz epsom salts
5-10 drops of essential oil (your choice of fragrance)

In a clean, dry container with a tight-fitting lid (or in a sealable bag), combine together all the ingredients and shake until well-mixed. Add 4-8 tablespoons to bathwater.

# SEA SALT BODY SCRUB

2 tablespoons fine sea salt
2 tablespoons cider vinegar
120ml/4fl oz flax oil or olive oil

In a small cup or bowl, mix the salt and vinegar together. Standing in the bath or shower (without water), rub yourself all over with oil. Gently massage in the pre-mixed salt mixture, paying attention to rough spots. Run a warm bath or shower and massage the oil and salt off your skin.

# DEODORANT DUSTING POWDER

50g/2oz cornflour
2-5 drops essential oil (your choice of fragrance)

In a clean, dry container with a tight-fitting lid (or in a sealable bag), combine ingredients and shake until well-mixed. Dust body, feet, and armpits with powder, using a duster, a soft cloth, or your hands.

## LIP GLOSS

4 tablespoons almond oil
3-4 tablespoons cocoa butter (solid), grated (the
   more cocoa butter you add, the harder the salve)
1-2 vitamin E capsules, pierced and drained

In a small saucepan on medium-low heat, heat the oil, cocoa butter, and vitamin E oil together until well-mixed. Pour into a small, clean, dry container and let cool. Once cool and set, cap tightly and use as needed. To make this as soft as petroleum jelly, add a bit more oil; to make it harder, add more cocoa butter.

## PERFUME

1 teaspoon essential oil (your choice of fragrance)
1 tablespoon almond oil

In a clean, dry bottle, pour ingredients and shake well before using. Good for up to 1 year.

## SOLID PERFUME

4 tablespoons almond oil
3-4 tablespoons cocoa butter (solid), grated (the
   more cocoa butter you add, the harder the salve)
1-2 vitamin E capsules, pierced and drained
7-15 drops of essential oil (your choice of fragrance)

In a small saucepan on medium-low heat, melt the oil, cocoa butter, vitamin E oil and fragrance together until well-mixed. Pour into a small, clean, dry bottle and let cool. Once cool and set, cap tightly and use as needed. To make this as soft as petroleum jelly, add a bit more oil; to make it harder, add more cocoa butter.

### Here are some scent combinations that you might want to try:

jasmine, patchouli
lavender, spearmint
sandalwood, musk, frankincense
sandalwood, musk, patchouli
lemon, spearmint, grapefruit
vanilla, musk
ginger, cinnamon, clove
strawberry, vanilla

# MASSAGE OIL

120ml/4fl oz oil (olive, almond, apricot, or sunflower)
10 drops essential oil (your choice of fragrance)

Pour oils into a clean, dry container. Cap tightly and shake well before using.

# ALL-PURPOSE SALVE

Use for insect bites, itching, wounds, minor skin abrasions, burns, bruises, tattoos, and on fungal infections.

Store salve in a dark-coloured jar so the light doesn't oxidise the herbs' healing properties. You can get these ingredients at health food or herb shops, or pick your own.

2 tablespoons St. John's wort*
2 tablespoons calendula*
2 tablespoons comfrey leaf*
2 tablespoons plantain*

250ml/8fl oz olive oil
1 tablespoon vitamin E oil
175-225g/6-8oz cocoa butter (solid), grated (the more cocoa butter you add, the harder the salve)

In a small pan, combine the herbs and oils. Simmer on low heat for about 4 hours to extract the beneficial properties of the herbs into the oil. Do not let oil get too hot. Once done, remove from heat and allow the oil to cool. Strain into a clean dry jar, using muslin or a sieve. Pour strained oil back into pot and add cocoa butter. On low heat, simmer until the cocoa butter is completely melted. Pour back into jar and let cool completely, then cap tightly.

* **St. John's wort**: good for burns, wounds, bites, itching, pain
* **Calendula**: anti-inflammatory; aids in healing abrasions; skin soother
* **Comfrey leaf**: speeds healing of wounds and skin conditions
* **Plantain**: pain relief; antiseptic for stings and bites

# BUG REPELLENT

250ml/8fl oz water
20 drops citronella oil
10 drops lavender essential oil
7 drops eucalyptus essential oil

In a spray bottle, combine all the ingredients and shake well. Spray exposed areas, but avoid face and eye area. To avoid possible irritation, try it out on a small patch of skin first.

# PEPPERMINT ITCH LOTION

For relief of itching.

120ml/4fl oz water
120ml/4fl oz witch hazel
3-4 drops peppermint or eucalyptus essential oil

In a clean, dry container, combine all the ingredients. Cap tightly and shake well. Apply to your skin with clean hands or cotton ball.

# SOOTHING SUNBURN LOTION

Always wear sunscreen and cover up as much as possible when you're outside in the sun. And keep your body well-hydrated by drinking plenty of water.

4 tablespoons water
2 tablespoons witch hazel
115g/4oz bicarbonate of soda
2-4 drops peppermint essential oil

In a clean, dry container, combine all the ingredients. Cap tightly and shake well. Gently apply to sunburned skin and allow to dry. This lotion will leave a fine, powdery film as it dries.

# CALENDULA BABY OIL

Calendula is healing and soothing to the skin. It is excellent for massaging your babies, but grown-ups can use this oil too!

250ml/8fl oz of oil (olive, almond, apricot, or
    sunflower)
2 1/2 tablespoons calendula flowers

In a small pot, combine the oil and flowers. Simmer on low heat for about 4 hours to extract the beneficial properties of the calendula into the oil. Do not let the oil get too hot. Once done, remove from heat and allow the oil to cool. Strain into a clean, dry container, using a muslin or sieve. Cap tightly.

# RE-USABLE BABY WIPES

4 tablespoons water
4 tablespoons animal-friendly shampoo
1 tablespoon vinegar
4 tablespoons aloe vera gel

1 tablespoon calendula oil (pg. 186)
1 drop lavender essential oil
1 drop tea tree oil

In a clean, dry jar, combine the water, shampoo, vinegar, aloe, calendula, lavender, and tea tree oil. Cap tightly, and shake well. Store in the fridge. Use soft but sturdy towels for wipes (flannel, old towels, etc.). Cut them into squares or rectangles and place them in a container with a tight lid. Pour solution over wipes. After using wipe, rinse thoroughly and wash in hot water in the washing machine, dry, and re-saturate with wipe solution. If your baby has a really red, raw nappy rash you might not want to use these wipes, as vinegar may cause a burning sensation.

# ANIMAL TREATS

These recipes are not for you, but for the ones who know you the best. They tolerate your tardiness, your mood swings, and your weird idiosyncrasies. They also love you no matter what you look like in the morning. Treat your animal friends well; they deserve only the best.

## DOG & CAT BISCUITS

115g/4oz wholemeal flour
2 tablespoons wheatgerm
10g/1/4 oz bran flakes
25g/1oz soy flour
1 tablespoon molasses
2 tablespoons oil

1 tablespoon kelp powder
1 teaspoon sage
1 tablespoon brewer's yeast
5 tablespoons water
2 tablespoons textured vegetable protein

Preheat oven to 180°C/350°F/gas mark 4. In a medium bowl, combine the flour, wheatgerm, bran flakes, soy flour, molasses, oil, kelp, sage, yeast, water, and TVP. Roll out and cut into shapes (for cats, roll out and cut into narrow strips or ribbons). Place on a baking sheet and bake for 20-35 minutes. Watch the kitty strips, as they will bake faster than the larger shapes. Cats like these biscuits soft, but dogs like them crunchy, so if the biscuits are not hard enough, leave them in the oven with the heat turned off until they reach the desired hardness. **Makes 12 large or 24 small biscuits.**

## CAROB CHIP-OATMEAL CRUNCHIES

50g/2oz oatmeal flour
25g/1oz soy bean flour
90g/3 1/2 oz rolled oat flakes
75g/3oz carob (do not use chocolate, it is toxic to dogs)

2 tablespoons textured vegetable protein
1 tablespoon brewer's yeast
4 tablespoons oil
4 tablespoons water (if too dry, add a little more)

Preheat oven to 180°C/350°F/gas mark 4. In a medium bowl, combine the flours, oats, carob, TVP, brewer's yeast, oil, and water. Roll out and cut into shapes. Place on a baking sheet and bake for 35-40 minutes. **Makes 12 large or 24 small crunchies.**

# BAD BREATH DOG BISCUITS

For some reason, my niece Heidi loves to eat these biscuits. It's so cute when she smiles and her teeth are green. **S**

225g/8oz wholemeal flour
50g/2oz cornmeal
20g/3/4 oz fresh mint, chopped
25g/1oz fresh parsley, chopped

1 teaspoon spirulina
2 tablespoons textured vegetable protein
175ml/6fl oz water
6 tablespoons oil

Preheat oven to 180°C/350°F/gas mark 4. In a medium bowl, combine the flour, cornmeal, mint, parsley, spirulina, TVP, water, and oil. Roll out and cut into shapes. Place on a baking sheet and bake for 35-40 minutes. **Makes 12 large or 24 small biscuits.**

# CORNMEAL CRUNCHIES DOG BISCUITS

225g/8oz wholemeal flour
50g/2oz cornmeal
2 tablespoons textured vegetable protein

1 tablespoon brewer's yeast
150ml/1/4 pint water
6 tablespoons oil

Preheat oven to 180°C/350°F/gas mark 4. In a medium bowl, combine the flour, cornmeal, TVP, yeast, water, and oil. Roll out and cut into shapes. Place on a baking sheet and bake for 35-40 minutes. **Makes 12 large or 24 small biscuits.**

# FLEA BUSTERS

Here are some ideas to prevent those nasty fleas:

**Brewer's yeast:** 1 teaspoon or 1 tablet a day. Note: some animals are allergic to brewer's yeast; watch for itchy patches. Consult your vet.
**Garlic:** Most animals love garlic when mixed into food.
**Calendula ointment or oil:** An excellent repellent that helps with itching.
**Vinegar:** A ratio of 1 teaspoon of vinegar to 1 litre/13/4 pints water in their drinking water helps to keep your pets free of fleas and ticks.

# FLEA HOUSE & PET SPRAY

Here is a natural way of eliminating fleas that is not harmful to humans or pets.

1/4 teaspoon eucalyptus or wintergreen essential oil     250ml/8fl oz water

Add oil to spray bottle filled with water. Spray your house with a fine mist – the carpet, furniture, car, pets' beds – everywhere. Fleas hate the aroma and run for cover. Spraying your pet is also a great idea. Spray areas 3 times a week all year round, but especially during summer, the peak flea season.

# Index